SOCIAL PROBLEMS
AND
SOCIAL POLICY:
The American Experience

SOCIAL PROBLEMS
AND
SOCIAL POLICY:
The American Experience

FAMILY CARE
OF
MENTAL PATIENTS

Editor
HORATIO M. POLLOCK

ARNO PRESS

A New York Times Company

New York — 1976

Editorial Supervision: SHEILA MEHLMAN

————◆————

Reprint Edition 1976 by Arno Press Inc.

Reprinted from a copy in the Pennsylvania State Library

SOCIAL PROBLEMS AND SOCIAL POLICY: The American Experience
ISBN for complete set: 0-405-07474-3
See last pages of this volume for titles.

Manufactured in the United States of America

————◆————

Library of Congress Cataloging in Publication Data

Pollock, Horatio Milo, 1868-1950, ed.
    Family care of mental patients.

    (Social problems and social policy--the American
experience)
    Reprint of the ed. published by State Hospitals Press,
Utica, N. Y.
    Bibliography: p.
    1. Mentally ill--United States--Home care.
2. Mentally ill--Europe--Home care.   I.   Title.
II.   Series.
RC443.P62 1976   362.2'4   75-17236
ISBN 0-405-07505-7

FAMILY CARE
OF
MENTAL PATIENTS

*A Review of Systems of Family Care in America
and Europe*

Editor
HORATIO M. POLLOCK, PH. D.,
NEW YORK STATE DEPARTMENT OF MENTAL HYGIENE, ALBANY, N. Y.

Contributors

EDGAR A. DOLL, Ph. D.,
THE TRAINING SCHOOL AT VINELAND, N. J.

HARRY A. LABURT, M. D.,
HARLEM VALLEY STATE HOSPITAL, WINGDALE, N. Y.

PHILIP SMITH, M. D.,
NEW YORK STATE DEPARTMENT OF MENTAL HYGIENE
NEW YORK CITY

CHARLES E. THOMPSON, M. D.,
GARDNER STATE HOSPITAL, EAST GARDNER, MASS.

CHARLES L. VAUX, M. D.,
NEWARK STATE SCHOOL, NEWARK, N. Y.

STATE HOSPITALS PRESS
UTICA, N. Y.
1936

To
Commissioner Frederick W. Parsons under
whose direction family care of mental patients
was instituted in New York State

FOREWORD

This is the first book written in the English language on the subject of family care of mental patients. Small treatises on the subject written in German and French have appeared, and a number of articles dealing with special topics relating to family care have been published from time to time in psychiatric journals. The present volume has been compiled to fulfill the need for a more comprehensive review of the whole theme.

The past two decades have witnessed an enormous expansion of institutional care of the mentally and physically sick, the defective, the delinquent and other classes of dependents. To meet the insistent demand for new institutions, large building programs have been undertaken, and in some cases when ordinary revenues failed to supply necessary funds, recourse was had to bond issues. New institutions when ready for occupancy are rapidly filled, and the demand for additional accommodations continues.

Naturally the question arises, Is there no way of escape from the heavy institutional burden that is now upon us and is becoming more oppressive year by year? Prevention and cure come first to mind as offering most promising forms of relief but with our present knowledge of prophylaxis and medical science, neither at present can afford us the necessary assistance. Some other means must be found. This book suggests family care as a supplement to, and a relief from, institutional care, and shows how this method of treatment is successfully carried on in many places in the United States and foreign countries.

The transformation already wrought in the care of dependent children gives an example of what may be accomplished in other fields. Foster family care has replaced institutional care of children to a large extent and is proving advantageous to the children placed, to the families receiving them and to the public generally. Unsupervised family care is now the only care available for the great majority of mental defectives and is still used to a large extent in the care of persons with mild forms of mental disease. These facts together with those showing the successful operation of systems of supervised family care lead to the conclusion that the latter affords practical means of relief from the institutional burden as well as a superior type of care for many of the unfortunate wards of the State.

The aim in the preparation of the book has been to present clear pictures of the various systems of family care, to show their advantages and disadvantages and to set forth the opinions of officials in immediate contact with patients and guardians. The editor has drawn freely from his addresses on family care previously published in Mental Hygiene and the American Journal of Psychiatry.

The editor expresses his appreciation and gratitude to those who have aided in the preparation of this volume, as follows:

To Dr. Edgar A. Doll, Dr. Charles E. Thompson, Dr. Philip Smith, Dr. Charles L. Vaux, and Dr. H. A. LaBurt for chapters contributed on various aspects of family care.

To Dr. A. J. Kilgour of Kingston, Ontario, for original photographs showing views of the Colony at Gheel.

To Dr. Gustav Kolb of Erlangen, Germany, for special information relating to the family care of mental patients in Germany.

To Dr. C. E. Farrar, for permission to republish material that had appeared in the American Journal of Psychiatry.

To Clifford W. Beers, for permission to quote from material published in the Proceedings of the International Congress on Mental Hygiene.

To Dr. Clarence M. Hincks, for permission to republish an article that originally appeared in Mental Hygiene.

HORATIO M. POLLOCK.

LIST OF ILLUSTRATIONS

CONTENTS

PART I. FAMILY CARE IN AMERICA

CHAPTER I

Introduction—Family Care of Mental Patients*

BY HORATIO M. POLLOCK

Systems and methods of care of mental patients have been discussed in this country for more than a century. For a long time progress was discouragingly slow. Cruel, heartless treatment gave way to humane custodial care only after long agitation and much misgiving. Such care was in turn superseded by scientific treatment only after another long period of discussion and trial. The modern hospital for the care of mental patients with its magnificent buildings, its trained personnel and elaborate medical equipment represents the culmination of the thought and effort of many decades. But the end is not yet. Science has entered the field and science is never satisfied. The scientific spirit spurs us on toward the discovery of new and better methods of medical treatment and of more economical and more efficient methods of care.

Necessity also has spurs and is beginning to use them. The ever-present conflict between what we want to do and what we are able to do is growing in intensity and is threatening the mental health

*Read at the ninetieth annual meeting of The American Psychiatric Association, New York City, May 28-June 1, 1934. Republished by permission of American Journal of Psychiatry.

of the nation.   Taxpayers groan under present burdens and are insistently demanding relief. The problem now before those vested with the care of mental patients is that of maintaining scientific standards while reducing per capita costs.

Economic changes of recent years have wrought havoc in our social order. With the possibility and the prospect of a better civilization with higher standards of living before us, we have been compelled to witness the decline of a large part of our population to a condition of idleness and poverty.   Modern machines enable us to produce much more than we can consume. From such abundance we would naturally expect bountiful living and a general advance in health, education, science and art. Unfortunately, just the opposite result is being experienced. Markets are flooded with products, labor is poorly employed. Income from securities is small. Rigid economy must be practiced by a large part of the population. New ways of making a living must be sought. Greater utilization of home resources for employment and means of income are everywhere receiving consideration. Hardest hit are the village and rural communities that have lost their industries. Some of these communities are reenacting the story so beautifully told in Goldsmith's ''Deserted Village.'' In the presence of these conditions it seems probable that many families in such communities would welcome the opportunity of rendering humanitarian service to the state by caring for mental patients for reasonable compensation.

Looking more closely into the present status of the care of mental patients in this country we find that about 400,000 patients with mental disease are being cared for in institutions. Of these, about 340,000 are in state hospitals and about 60,000 in other institutions. The present annual rate of increase of patients in state hospitals is about 4½ per cent. With this rate compounded for 50 years we can easily compute the institutional load our grandchildren would have to carry. Unfortunately, the increase of mental patients is cumulative and the annual rate is increasing. While we are waiting and hoping for a change of trend it behooves us to make provision for the inevitable increase of the next few years.

If mental patients were the only dependents to be cared for by the state the matter would be comparatively simple; but the resources of public treasuries have already proved inadequate to meet the demands made upon them. Even our wealthier states have been obliged to float large bond issues for public relief and for the erection of new buildings for mental patients and other classes of dependents. Naturally there arises the question as to whether new ways and means of lessening the burden of dependency cannot be devised.

To provide for the increase of mental patients we must either build new hospitals or make arrangements for the care of part of the patients outside of hospitals. The problem we are facing is similar to that which has obtained in Germany ever since the World War. In that country means have not been available for the construction of many new hospitals. Hospital care has therefore been supplemented by placing patients in families for small compensation or by keeping patients under supervision in their own homes. This system of family care adopted by necessity is found to be giving a high degree of satisfaction. The patients receive adequate care and the families caring for them are thereby placed in a better economic position.

The question of organization of systems of family care to supplement institution care is being seriously considered in this country. It is probable that in the near future several states will join Massachusetts and New York in using family care for at least a small number of selected patients.

To aid us in determining what kind of family care is best, we have many examples before us. It is well known that at the famous colony at Gheel in Belgium mental patients have been successfully cared for in homes of both villagers and farmers for several centuries; that Scotland has placed patients in isolated families for 80 years or more; that France, Sweden and Switzerland use family care for a part of their mental patients; that Mass-

achusetts, since 1885, has conducted family care
of patients on a small scale; and that in nearly
every state of this country unrecovered mental patients are placed on parole either with their own
relatives or with other families. There is, therefore, no question about the feasibility or desirabil-
ity of certain types of family care.

In introducing a system of family care consider-
tion must be given to the welfare of patients, the
expense involved, the means to be taken to secure
adequate supervision, the conditions to be met to
obtain public approval and the general welfare of
the community in which the patients are placed.
The system in use in Scotland by which the insane
are cared for in widely separated homes has, on
the whole, little to commend it to Americans. It
may be economical and it is possible that the patients as a whole may be well cared for, but proper
supervision of such care cannot be exercised and
the system seems ill-adapted for large scale placement. The system developed by Dr. Kolb at Erlangen, Germany, by which patients in homes are
kept under the immediate supervision of the state
hospital seems better than the Scottish system but
does not seem adapted for extensive use in this
country. The system at Gheel though far from
ideal presents many features which could be
adopted with suitable modifications in the organization of systems of family care in this country.*

*See Chapters VII, VIII and IX.

In the light of the experience thus far gained it would seem feasible to attempt the establishment of special colonies of the Gheel type in selected country villages in this country. The colony of the sort I am visualizing would have a central community house with emergency hospital facilities for a few patients. This community house would be the headquarters of the physician in charge of the colony and of the social workers, nurses, occupational therapists, and others who would supervise the patients placed in family care. The community house would serve as an intermediate station between the state hospital and the families receiving patients. Patients would go from the state hospital to the community house and from there to their family home. If it became necessary to return a patient placed in family care, he would be sent first to the community house and then either to another family or back to the state hospital. The community house would also serve as a social center for the patients of the colony.

The number of patients that could be economically placed by a single center would depend on several factors including the willingness of the people residing in the community to receive patients, the number of available families and the number of available patients. In some village communities it is probable that 1,000 patients might be placed without great difficulty. With others the number might be as low as 100 or 200. The system would necessarily start with small beginnings and would develop gradually until a large group was reached.

A colony might be started by placing a certain number of patients directly from the hospital and later establishing a community house, or a community house might first be established and patients placed out from such house as rapidly as found expedient. If the project were undertaken it should be preceded by active propaganda showing the benefits to be derived from family care, the opportunities offered to families to render humanitarian service and the advantage to be derived by the state and the community from the introduction of the system.

In beginning a state system of family care it might be expedient to start with the placing of mental defectives as Dr. Charles L. Vaux of the Newark State School is doing in the village of Walworth, N. Y.* It is believed that mental defectives might be more easily placed than mentally diseased patients and would not be quite so difficult to manage. If a colony were started and developed into a large undertaking such as here projected it would serve as an example to other communities and the success attending the first colony would aid greatly in the establishment of other colonies.

Good judgment must be exercised in selecting patients for family care. In a mental hospital, patients suitable for placing out include quiet schizo-

*See Chapter III.

2

phrenic cases, chronic manic-depressives, and other undisturbed types that are tractable and capable of following instructions. These, in some hospitals, would include a third of all resident patients.

Types not suitable for family care include the following:

1. Patients with acute disorders who are likely to recover within a few months.

2. Patients that are noisy, destructive, violent or suicidal.

3. Patients that are bedridden or that require constant medical and nursing care.

4. Patients that are undergoing special medical or psychiatric treatment.

5. Patients that are contentious or have pronounced delusions of persecution.

6. Patients with marked erotic tendencies.

7. Patients that have severe convulsions.

The care of infirm patients in private homes would be possible only if special facilities were provided. It is probable that if standards of care were not made too high many families might desire to establish nursing homes for infirm patients. In these homes the state hospitals might place patients whose relatives would be willing to pay $10 to $15 per week for their care but could not afford the higher rates charged by well-equipped licensed institutions. It is, of course, conceivable that a

nursing home might be a large institution rather
than a family affair. However, I see no good reason why a family having a spacious home could not
use it for a nursing home to accommodate as few
as five or six patients. Already many such nursing homes are in use for the care of the infirm and
neurotic who are not classed as psychotic. If state
encouragement were given these homes their number would multiply and the state hospitals would
be correspondingly relieved.

The financial side of family care deserves most
careful consideration. It is probable that the rate
to be paid for the board of patients should not be
uniform. Women patients who are able and willing to help with housework and men patients who
would render service in the garden or on the farm
would be placed at a much cheaper rate than patients who are unable to work. Patients requiring
a great deal of personal supervision should be paid
for at a higher rate than those able to care for
themselves.

In general, family care should be much less
costly than hospital care. The latter varies widely
in different parts of the country. In northern
states providing good medical and nursing service
in well-equipped hospitals, the per capita cost of
care of mental patients amounts to nearly $12 per
week. This amount includes cost of housing and
administration as well as cost of maintenance.
Housing cost alone in the newer hospitals amounts

to approximately $5 per week. If a system of family care were instituted it seems probable that the housing charge could be saved and the entire expense of maintaining patients in family care could be defrayed by a total per capita expenditure of from $5 to $7 per week. At this rate a substantial saving would result.

The advantages derived from family care are four-fold: Patients placed in suitable families resume a measure of community life with a natural environment and with more freedom than could be possible in a state hospital. The families receiving patients have an outlet for their altruistic sentiments and acquire a secure economic status. The state hospital relieved of many of its custodial cases can devote more of its energies to the scientific treatment of acute and recoverable patients. The state conducting an extensive system of family care would be relieved of the necessity of building new hospitals and would have a better opportunity to treat its mental patients in accordance with their individual needs.

CHAPTER II

Family Care of the Insane in Massachusetts

BY CHAS. E. THOMPSON, M D.,

SUPERINTENDENT, GARDNER STATE HOSPITAL, EAST GARDNER, MASS.

In presenting the history of family care of the insane in Massachusetts, it is necessary to go back 75 years to about the year 1860 to a period when matters of public welfare were demanding attention and the question of how best to meet them are of record. In doing this, one is struck by the similarity of the questions of those days with those of today; far less in size but similar in importance.

From the earliest time in Massachusetts the family has been considered the essential unit of society. All matters of policy gave special consideration to the family unit. Home care for the handicapped was early stressed. It was believed that more could be accomplished thereby for the individual and the family. It is, therefore, to be expected that in those early days much thought would have been given to the value of life in the home in the care of the sick and the handicapped, whether it were the child, the poor, the blind or the mentally ill.

Prior to the middle of the last century, problems of health of the body or the mind, had not received special attention except as problems of individuals, and because of the sparse, isolated population, they were not of sufficient importance to require special community attention or anything like State supervision. Matters relating to pauperism and crime, doubtless influenced by mental defect or mental disease, had been, from the time of the first settlers, matters of community concern.

As the population of the Commonwealth increased, the matter of relief became more and more pressing and finally about 1860 it seemed necessary to consider a central State authority which would have supervision over matters of relief, and that the various charitable activities should be correlated and supervised.

In 1863 a State Board of Charities was established, this being the first board of its kind in this country. To this first board of charity, men of broad interests and understanding were appointed. From our point of view in considering the family care of the insane, the two most outstanding of these were Frank B. Sanborn of Concord, who was appointed to the Board in 1863, becoming secretary of the Board and serving until 1875; and Dr. Samuel G. Howe appointed in 1863, becoming chairman of the Board in 1865 and continuing in office until 1874. These two were the fathers of the family-care system in Massachusetts. They were outstanding in their interest and in their understanding of the mentally retarded and mentally ill. Their studies and reports had much to do with the subsequent establishment of the family-care system in Massachusetts.

Mr. Sanborn was interested in all matters relating to public welfare and affairs militant during the Civil War both in this and other states. His active interest in legislative matters in the organization and the conduct of boards relating to welfare matters continued well into the present century.

Dr. Howe was particularly interested in the blind and through his efforts the first school for the blind in this country was established. His interest also was in the need of training of defective children which interest resulted in the establishment of the first school for the feebleminded in this country. His interest in the insane continued throughout his active life.

These facts are mentioned to stress the standing of these men in matters of public welfare. They both had visited other countries and had studied the systems of family care in use there, especially that at Gheel, Belgium.

The early annual report of the State Board of Charity, established in 1863, contained ideas fully as pertinent and significant today as when written 70 years ago. Important then, but many times as important today. Many principles enunciated then are applicable now. Many of the questions regarding family care of the insane that we are discussing today seem to have been discussed from a similar point of view in the early reports of the board. It, therefore, does not seem amiss to quote rather fully from these early reports as they relate to this subject.

In the first report of 1864 considerable discussion appeared as to the increasing number of insane and the probable future increase. There were in Massachusetts three hospitals for the insane. The report stated:

These institutions in their construction and management were designed for hospitals in which insane persons were to be treated, if possible cured. They were provided with every means, medical, physical and mental as was calculated to have salutary and remedial influence on mind and body in a deranged state. Such means and accommodations cannot be other than expensive, not only the first cost, but keeping them up from year to year. These hospitals were never intended to be receptacles or permanent homes for the harmless or incurable insane who can derive no benefit whatever from hospital treatment. Little more can be done for this class than to surround them with proper restraint and to supply their physical wants. Neither justice nor humanity requires the State to spend large sums of money on persons who cannot be benefited thereby.

In this first report is also mentioned a plan proposed by Dr. William Prince who was the first superintendent of the Northampton State Hospital at its opening in 1858. Dr. Prince writes in his report for the year 1862 the following:

The already enormous expense of supportng so large a number of insane foreign paupers would cause our tax payers to receive with great disfavor any proposition to

increase the number of institutions or to increase at any
considerable expense the accommodations now existing.
And yet, before the lapse of many years, something will
be required, and perhaps a judicious system of coloniza-
tion, as practiced in some European countries, may be
found equally beneficial to the patient and the treasury
of the Commonwealth. That these patents are not entirely unproductive, as a class, the industrial statistics
of some institutions clearly show. The amount of labor
performed in some of these, if the figures are reliable,
is quite remarkable, and strongly suggestive of the idea
that, by proper selection of cases, proper care and super-
intendence, in suitable localities, under a suitable system
of general supervision, much might be done to develop a
latent element of profit by fanning into life the now dormant and fading spark of usefulness in these truly piti-
able sons and daughters of misfortune. A few trials, entirely experimental, made during the year now closed,
lead to the belief that much good, with little risk, would
result from a carefully conducted series of experiments
in this direction under suitable skillful supervision.

Dr. Pliny Earle followed Dr. Prince as superintendent of the Northampton State Hospital. Dr.
Earle in a paper published in 1851 in the American
Journal of Insanity, Volume VIII, described his
visit to Gheel, Belgium, his description being one
of the earliest on record in this country. In this
description he states that it was a question whether
the welfare of the insane was as much promoted in
Gheel as it would be in asylums or hospitals. This,
he stated, had recently been discussed in Belgium,
particularly by medical men and public officers who
maintained that patients under their care enjoy
greater liberty and suffer less coercion while they

breathe the pure air and take more exercise. When more constantly under supervision, by being so widely distributed, a few in each family, they are less subjected to disturbance and annoyance from other patients than is possible in large institutions. He stated that he saw nothing in Gheel that would tend to excite his doubt that patients were kindly treated by their immediate protectors. He felt, however, that the system was liable to greater abuse than could possibly occur in a well-ordered institution. Dr. Earle's doubt, however, seems to have given way after further study of the family care system of Scotland and Belgium and he heartily approved in 1865 and the following years of the introduction of the Scottish system into Massachusetts, even selecting himself a few of the old cases who were to be boarded out from the Northampton State Hospital.

In January, 1890, at the age of 90 he joined with Dr. Talbot of Boston, Mr. Allen of Medfield, Mr. Barrus, trustee of the Northampton State Hospital, and others in recommending that there should be established in Massachusetts a qualified commission that should in part, "provide for the chronic insane in asylums and families."

It appears that other superintendents favored a trial of the family care system. Dr. W. B. Goldsmith, superintendent of the Danvers State Hospital, writes in 1884:

A small number of carefully selected patients can properly be boarded out in private families. The class of families which are suitable to care for such charges in this country, are usually not to be tempted by the small rate paid for dependent patients but it would be economical for the State to increase this rate if necessary as all expenses for construction would be avoided when a case is so provided for. Although any beginning in this direction would be small, if cases were carefully selected and judiciously pushed, the practice would be likely to spread from family to family and I have little doubt but that after a few years several hundred of the insane would be thus cared for economically on the part of the State and comfortably for themselves.

The second annual report of the State Board of Charity, 1865, mentions a meeting of the Association of Superintendents of Insane Hospitals at Pittsburg, Pa., in June, 1864, at which meeting a plan was presented by Dr. Hill of West Virginia recommending that farms or a hamlet of houses for the chronic insane be established on the village style. In this report much was made of the opportunity in homes for the chronic insane stressing the desirable features of gardening, agricultural pursuits and the lighter trades and manufactures.

In the third annual report of 1886 mention is made that Dr. Bemis of the Worcester State Hospital had recommended that a hospital be established in the central part of the State where would be located the "hospital proper" with every facility for treating all cases of acute mania and for all violent, suicidal, dangerous and troublesome cases and nearby a few plain, neat substantial cottages capable of accommodating a family of eight or ten quiet, harmless, industrious persons. Dr. Bemis also recommended that not far removed from these, two or three houses be erected of somewhat more style and somewhat more pretentious for a class of people found in every hospital where they could live in quiet families. It was suggested that these houses be in charge of old and well-trained attendants who would find there inducement to remain and take care of the insane, making it a life business.

The State Board expressed its opinion of this as follows:

The great benefit, it seems to us, to be derived from the wide departure of accustomed rules, is a near approach to the family system and the kindly influence of home treatment.

The Board further expressed itself:

Could this system or some similar one be carried into operation, the insane would have all the advantages they now have with the added advantage of the family circle for such as could be admitted to enjoyment, homely surroundings and the enjoyment of many social comforts which make life pleasant. They would also have the advantage of well-trained educated nurses and attendants whose business for life would be to care for and sympathize with them. They would enjoy a more free style of recreation and exercise with less restraint and would mingle in the society of relatives and friends.

In a word: All enjoyments of life would be multiplied and all social endearments to a very great extent preserved without diminishing in any way the prospects of recovery or increasing the labors of the institution.

Home in Town of South Royalston, Mass., in Which Patients Have Been Cared
for 28 Years

A Finnish Home at Gardner, Mass., in Which Two Finnish Patients Live

The suggestion made by Dr. Bemis seems to refer to the development of colonies adjacent to existing hospitals, rather more than to family care.

The fourth annual report of the State Board of 1867 laid down "General Principles of Charitable Administration," as follows:

1.   That it is better to separate and diffuse the dependent classes than to congregate them.

2.   That we ought to avail ourselves as much as possible of those remedial agencies which exist in society; the family, social influences, industrial occupations and the like.

3.   That we should enlist, not only the greatest amount of popular sympathy but the greatest number of individuals and families in the care and treatment of dependents.

4.   That we should avail ourselves of responsible societies and organizations which aim to reform, support or help any class of dependents thus lessening the direct agency of the State and enlarging that of the people themselves.

5.   That we should build up public institutions only as a last resort and that these should be as small as is consistent with a wise economy.

The second is of special importance, that public charity should promote unity and integrity of families and enlist the greatest possible number of families in the work which it has to do. The board holds that family treatment, as a rule, would be better:

1.   For the wards themselves.

2.   For those who have charge of them.

3.   For the Commonwealth.

It would be almost a waste of words to attempt to show how much better it would be for the wards themselves to be cared for in private families, rather than in public institutions. It would, as a general rule, be better for those who have charge of the wards, if they could live in ordinary homesteads and better for their families to have them do so.

There exists in certain parts of Massachusetts an abundance of womanly energy and capacity which is unemployed and dormant. By a wise and discriminate arrangement gradually introduced, much of the work of training and caring for the infirm in mind as well as body which is now attempted by aggregating the subjects at a few points in large establishments might be done by distributing them in suitable families in various parts of the country with more advantage to themselves and to the community.

The family treatment will be better for the Commonwealth. The average Massachusetts families are intelligent and very apt to learn. They will improve by every opportunity and by practice will become more skillful and successful in managing the persons committed to them as wards.

Inasmuch as this State Board in 1867 made its first recommendation to the Legislature regarding family care, it is of interest to record their reasons:

A PLAN PROPOSED FOR TREATING THE CHRONIC INSANE

We commend to the attention of the Legislature these suggestions: That a certain number of the chronic insane now in the State hospitals be sent to their respective homes and that a small allowance be made to their families for their support. We are strongly inclined to the opinion that the system of selecting a certain number of chronic and harmless insane and placing them in families be adopted as part of the State policy and we recommend that the experiment be tried.

If the principle should be adopted it would bring relief in many cases, although the allowance made to families should be less than the present actual cost to the

State. There are in the remote parts of the State families where the material condition is such as to make some arrangement of this kind desirable, both for the sake of having an honorable and useful occupation and for the profit it would bring. In many cases that might decide the doubt as to whether many families could be kept together, the old homestead preserved or not.

It would be useless to set forth at length the moral and material advantages that would follow a successful trial of this plan. It provides relief to the hospital and an increase of their remedial power over recent cases which the removal of chronic cases would bring. It would provide joy to patients, not too demented to be sighing for freedom, beside the comfort it would give to a relative at finding their lost one restored to comparative freedom. This step would be an important one toward the end which should ever be in view, namely the reduction of the number and extent of aggregations of sufferers in hospitals, by making provisions for the greatest possible number of the infirm and dependents by the hands of those who are well and strong, in ordinary habitants.

RECOMMENDATION TO THE LEGISLATURE (1867)

We would recommend the policy of placing a portion of harmless insane in private dwellings, at the expense of the public, instead of permitting them to accumulate in hospitals or asylums to the exclusion of more recent and curable cases.

Under careful supervision, we believe that a certain number of this class of indigent insane would best be provided for with comfort to themselves and economy to the public. This plan would not involve the building of costly or even cheap structures for their reception. Patients of this class might be sent out from the hospitals, or permitted to remain where many of them now are, or soon will be, in their own families, or some other suitable place outside of the hospital.

Each year following this declaration of principles as recommended to the Legislature of 1867, further mention was made by the State Board in its report of the need of a family-care system.

The sixth annual report of 1884 contained a report made by Dr. Henry R. Stedman, former assistant superintendent of the Danvers State Hospital, who had travelled abroad studying the family-care system of foreign countries, particularly that of Scotland. This report, in part, stressed the experience of Dr. Clouston and his recommendation of the boarding-out system as follows:

Dr. Clouston, superintendent of one of the foremost asylums in Scotland says:

'When the patients become quiet and chronic, I select them and send their names to the Inspector of the Poor who finds suitable guardians. Of late years since it (the boarding system) was better understood, better organized and better supervised, the results have been good on the whole and very good in some cases. Money has been saved, patients have been sufficiently well cared for and in many cases made happier. The asylums have been relieved from overcrowding, prevented from growing unmanageable in size and have been left more to their proper work of treating the curable and recent cases.

'I cannot imagine any country where a certain proportion and a certain kind of chronic and quiet lunatics and imbeciles should not be boarded out in private houses. Asylum life is at its best an unnatural and expensive thing and in my opinion its undoubted benefit to most cases of insanity do not apply to certain of the more quiet and manageable patients.'

The need of a law establishing a family-care system was annually stressed by the State Board and finally resulted in the Acts of 1885, Chapter 385.

An Act Providing for the Care of Certain Insane Persons

Be it enacted, as follows:

Section 1. The State Board of Health, Lunacy and Charity is hereby authorized to place to board where they deem it expedient, and in suitable families throughout the Commonwealth, insane persons of the chronic, quiet class, the cost of boarding such insane persons having no settlement, shall be paid from the appropriation of the Board of State Paupers and Lunatic Hospitals; but the rate paid for their board shall not exceed the rate now paid in the State Lunatic Hospitals.

Section 2. (Has to do with the method of payment of bills.)

Section 3. It shall be the duty of the Board of Health, Lunacy and Charity to cause all insane persons who are boarded in families at the expense of the Commonwealth to be visited at least once in three months. All insane persons who are boarded in families at the expense of towns and cities and whose residence is made known to such Board, shall be visited in like manner, once in six months by proper agents of the Board.

Section 4. (Gave permit to remove to and from hospital and family.)

Section 5. This act shall take effect upon its passage.

Approved June 19, 1885.

It is to be noticed that the State Board of Charity had in 1878 become the State Board of Health, Lunacy and Charity.

3

This act went into effect on the 18th of July. Thirty days after its enactment, on the 10th of August, 1885, two State patients were sent to boarding places under its provision. This number was increased to 29 by the first of January, 1886. It was not thought best to try the experiment of boarding out patients on a large scale until the results of a cautious trial had been ascertained, there being much doubt in the minds of many people concerning the safety and general expediency of such a policy.

The eighth annual report of the Board of 1886 indicates that the insane in families received much discussion by the public. Reference in that report is made to the fact that the small private asylum derives much of its advantage from the fact that it gives patients something similar to family care, not separating them entirely from ordinary social life. It was felt that this advantage was also to be gained by boarding the insane in good families.

Sixty persons had been boarded out in the three-year period following the passing of the law of 1885 as amended by Chapter 319, 1886. The results were on the whole satisfactory. About two-thirds of those placed in families were women. At least two of those placed in family care in the first few years of its adoption still remain in family care today, 1935. One placed in 1888 still remaining in family care was visited recently by the writer. Although advanced in years, this patient holds Mr. Sanborn in grateful remembrance, expressing her appreciation that he found her a home away from the hospital. Her one expressed wish is that she be not returned to any hospital. Another patient placed in 1889 was also recently visited. While quite old and feeble and with fading memories, she was quite happy and it was strikingly shown that the other patients in this family were very solicitous of her welfare and comfort.

As years have passed, changes have been made in the supervising Board. The State Board of Health, Lunacy and Charity of 1878 was divided in 1886, two Boards being established, the State Board of Lunacy and Charity and the State Board of Health. In 1898 this Board was divided and two Boards established, the State Board of Insanity and the State Board of Charity. In 1916 the State Board of Insanity became the Commission on Mental Diseases and in 1919 the present Department of Mental Diseases.

The family-care system has been continued by each State Board. There has, however, been a growing tendency to consider the family-care system a hospital function rather than a departmental one. From 1885 to 1905, all patients were boarded out by the central Board. In 1905 the statues extended the privilege of placement to the State hospitals. During the years from 1901 to 1914 the State Board employed a medical director and two social workers who gave their entire time to the se-

lection, placement and supervision of patients
boarded in families. In 1915 the Board discontinued its own selection and placement, transfer-
ring many of those in foster homes to the supervision of the hospitals. In 1933 the Department
of Mental Diseases believing the boarding-out system to be primarily a hospital function transferred
all those remaining to the supervision of the State
hospitals. The provision of the law, Section 19,
Chapter 123, requiring the Department of Mental
Diseases to visit all patients in family care was re-
pealed in 1935. At the present time all patients
are selected and placed by the hospitals, the family care being an integral part of each hospital and
under its sole supervision.

At the present time, October, 1935, 317 patients
are cared for in foster homes by 11 hospitals. They
are located in 44 different towns and cities of the
Commonwealth. The cost is governed by statute.
If State supported at a sum not exceeding $4.50
per week per patient exclusive of clothing and supervision. Appropriations for this purpose are re-
quested and granted as an item under general medical care.

The period of the greatest activity and the largest number under care in foster homes was from
1901 to 1915, the largest number being placed when
supervision was given by a medical officer of the
central Board. In 1901 there were 117 in foster
homes. This number increased each year until

Home in Town of Royalston, Mass, in Which Four Patients Are Members **of** a Family

Fairview Cottage Colony, Gardner State Hospital. A Half-way Station Between Hospital and Home

1914 when there were 341. In 1915 following discontinuance of selection by the central Board, a slight increase was noticed but a gradual annual decline then followed. A part of the reason for this was doubtless the effect of the World War and conditions following for several years. Since 1931 the number has again shown a gradual increase and homes for placement are more readily obtained.

Dr. Pliny Earle of the Northampton State Hospital, as early as 1890 drew attention to the fact that family care might well be provided for the convalescent patient as well as the chronic.

OCCUPATIONAL THERAPY CENTER AT CITY MILLS

An interesting and very unusual step in the development of family care in mental cases was the establishment of an occupational therapy center in 1922 by the Boston State Hospital, James V. May, M. D., superintendent, under the supervision of the Massachusetts Department of Mental Diseases. This center is now located at City Mills, Mass. It has the benefit of the suggestions and supervision of an advisory board composed of prominent ladies of the city of Boston who have taken a tremendous interest in it from its conception.

The location as shown above is in a very attractive community only 20 miles from Boston. The object of the undertaking was to provide a community center for cases that have improved to such an extent as to warrant their leaving the hospital and taking up a residence outside in a place where they can be under supervision until they have succeeded in readjusting themselves to their environment and are able to return to their own homes or support themselves. The key to this possible readjustment would appear to be the resumption of occupational interests. With this purpose in mind, the patients at City Mills have the benefit of instruction from a competent and experienced occupational therapist. Patients are visited at frequent intervals by one of the physicians from the hospital keeping in touch with both their physical and mental conditions.

The articles made by the patients are disposed of at an annual sale in which they, naturally, take a great deal of interest. Under the direction of a housekeeper and her husband who have immediate supervision of the building, the patients are also interested in housework and various activities.

Family Care for the Convalescing

Recently the Worcester State Hospital, William A. Bryan, M. D., superintendent, extended the family-care system at that hospital to include the convalescing in the belief that the boarding home becomes not a permanent residence but a stepping stone to mental health, independence and self-support. With these possibilities in mind, the psychiatric staff of that hospital is now referring for boarding home placement only such patients as may be aided in their social recovery by such placement.

Special emphasis is placed upon the selection of the home and the fitting of the patient in the home endeavoring to find the right kind of situation for each patient. In general it has been found that the schizophrenics make their best adjustment in a simple home situation. Depressed patients become more unhappy in a home where there are people coming and going, creating excitement and confusion. Attempt is made to improve the standards of some of the patients by placing them in homes of a similar level to those they were formerly accustomed to but each patient placed governs this.

In general the placing of convalescing patients requires special effort on the part of the social service department and a development of greater understanding on the part of friends and it has been found that in the choice of the home, family and caretaker, personality and understanding are more important than physical surroundings in creating a therapeutic situation. "It is a fundamental principle that no patient remain longer in a convalescent home than is necessary to prepare him to take his place in his family or industrial group."

As stated in a report from this hospital it is felt

that the psychotherapeutic value of boarding homes for mental patients is considerably greater than is commonly supposed, and for this reason, boarding homes should be utilized more widely, provided skilled social service supervision can be given.

The family-care system is in use by each of the 11 hospitals for the mentally ill in Massachusetts, although the numbers placed from each are not large but are increasing.

To describe the family care system in some detail, as it is now in use requires that I describe it as carried on at the Gardner State Hospital.

This hospital corresponds, in many respects, to the German system. Established as an occupational institution for the mentally ill and developed on the village plan it has its hospital center for administration, facilities for the reception of new cases and for those requiring hospital treatment, while scattered over wide areas are colonies of simpler construction and administration. For those of the continued care type organized occupational therapy and practical adult occupations are provided in all departments. The natural extension of this occupation colony has been the development of a family-care department.

When the State board discontinued its selection and placement of patients in 1915, we continued this work. At the end of the first year, 29 patients were residing in families in this community. The plan has been continued as an important part of our organization and at the present time we have 106 residing in 22 different homes in the surrounding rural community. The number in each family varies from two to six. The average is 3.8. Six are placed in a family only under unusual circumstances. The total number placed has been limited only by the appropriation granted for this particular purpose. We are asking for a larger appropriation for the coming year that a larger number may be placed in foster homes.

As provided by statute we pay in most instances $4.50 per week and supply clothing and supervision. A few are privately supported.

Organization

A staff physician has immediate supervision as a part of her extramural work. The entire time of this physician is devoted to community needs including clinics; study of backward children in public schools, child guidance, habit clinics, consultations, etc. Associated with her are three social workers, one of whom gives most of her time to family care.

Caretakers are selected very carefully. References must be good; location desirable, physical properties of the home satisfactory.

Patients selected as suitable by staff physicians are presented at staff meeting for consideration before placement. Those selected by us are largely of the middle age and upward group. We have avoided placement of the young, although there have been exceptions. Fewer dangers present themselves after middle life and family care, it seems to us, grows more attractive with advancing years of a patient.

Patients are visited frequently by the physicians, social workers, personal hygienist, occupational therapist, dentist and by the pastors of the parish. Caretakers are required to confer promptly as questions arise and occasionally visit the hospital singly or in a group for instruction and general discussion that all may be fully informed as to our standards of general care.

Prior to 1921 the rate of board paid was $3.75 per week. This amount was lower than prevailing prices in other endeavors and it was not easy to find suitable homes. Since 1921 the rate of $4.50 per week has been paid and with the prevailing lessening of industrial activities, families are requesting more patients than we are able to place with the money provided. We now pay $4.50 per week which is somewhat less than the hospital weekly per capita. In 1932 the weekly per capita cost of family care was $1.05 less; in 1933, 44 cents less; in 1934 it was 31 cents less; in 1935, $1.37* less. The per capita cost for family care remains practically stationary each year while that of the hospital varies. The cost of supervision, distance

*These comparisons take no account of the investment charge for hospital plant.

traveled, medical care, etc., added to the amount paid for board gives us the comparative cost as stated.

At this hospital we believe in the family-care system as a department of the hospital and believe it may be still further developed. We believe it to be of benefit to the patient, that it is of community value, that it relieves overcrowding, that its economic aspect recommends it.

We here believe family care to be a benefit to a certain number and type of mental patients for whom the hospital offers little hope of bringing about recovery. Continued hospitalization does in practice no more for them than to offer kindly, comfortable care which may be even better provided in selected homes in the community. This presupposes that the majority placed are of an older age group. There are, however, undoubtedly, many of a younger age for whom community care would contribute more than will a hospital. Careful selection must be made and suitable training and follow-up provided.

We believe family care to be of community value. It can hardly fail to benefit the caretakers and neighbors. We know from experience that they become attached to their patients just as we do within the hospital. They enjoy and are benefited by frequent contacts with the hospital, contacts which many of them have never had before. A number of our caretakers, however, are former

employees. We note in the caretakers a broad-
ened view of persons and things. Improvement,
perhaps in their own personal appearances, tidi-
ness of the home, etc. Caretakers who are of the
acceptable type cannot maintain standards required by the hospital without thereby having
their own standards raised by the supervision and
encouragement given them. It is a common thing
to learn of unusual things done by the caretakers
for the patients purely because of their interest
and attachment.

It is our experience that the caretakers and
neighbors show more sincere interest in, more
helpfulness toward their patients, than do many
relatives. We do not pay relatives for the care of
their own, believing that, while this might be indicated in occasional instances, as a practice it would
not be wise. Those patients who have relatives are
discharged to them. The majority of our patients
in foster homes have no relatives financially able
to assist them and are not patients who may be discharged to the community unsupervised and un-
aided.

At present in some states the portion of the state
tax required to maintain hospitals is larger than
that of any other activity. Hospitals have more
than doubled their capacity in the past 25 years.
Considering this fact the family-care system would
seem to offer relief.

It is, however, neither the increasing numbers under care nor the question of the types of buildings thought necessary that is the important question. Most important of all is what is best for the individual. The hospital is built around the individual needing care. Any individual is, naturally, most happy in home surroundings. To those of our patients who may be returned to home surroundings, even to foster homes, comes a feeling of freedom regained, at least in part, a relief from the crowded, unhappy surroundings of the hospital, the sharing of home life, the opportunity of doing the things one likes to do, the opportunity to enjoy the out of doors. In rural communities there are usually gardens, for flowers, for vegetables for home consumption, doubtless a cow or two, hens, domestic pets and an expanse of land on which they may roam. There are the duties of the home to be attended to and at night, not a dormitory shared with many, with unavoidable disturbances and subdued light, but one's own room or a room shared with one or two others; bathing privacy even though primitive; the opportunity to enjoy the privacy of one's toilet even though it may be lacking the last word in plumbing; the opportunity for personal care, to have access to one's own clothing and belongings. These are only a few of the desirable features of home life that contrast it to that of a hospital. The important thing is that one is an individual, not one of hundreds and is offered the opportunity of sharing the joy of home life.

There are always some things which those who have lived in an institution for a considerable period miss, not only in family care but upon discharge. The weekly or occasional entertainment, movies, dances, church, having everything done for them. Time is necessary to bring about readjustment to home life in any case whether in a patient or a hospital employee after separation from hospital life, but this is to be expected. Time must be allowed for such readjustment.

There are the questions: Are patients well cared for? Are the foster homes likely to exploit them? Are patients overworked? Will they be well fed? The answer to these and similar pertinent doubts is a question largely of careful selection of homes, painstaking and intelligent supervision and visitation by those appointed for this work by the hospital. It is important that these visitors know the patient while at the hospital and that the patients know the visitor and fully understand the advantages and the requirements of family care. During this pre-family care period a friendly understanding is arrived at so that on subsequent visits to the home and in private conversation, always insisted upon, the true situation may be easily learned.

One naturally asks why anyone having a home would wish to take mental patients into it. Is it not solely an opportunity to make money? If so, is it to be expected that patients will be as well cared for in the home as at the hospital? These are most natural and important questions. Usually the reason given us by applicants for boarding patients is that they have unused rooms and an increased income is desired. There may be no market for their farm products, etc., etc. It is quite often because the wife is anxious to assist and to have some work and interest. It is our experience that an increased income is the real desire in most cases on the part of the family but it is not our experience that the patients are exploited, ill fed or improperly cared for. An instance here and there of this has been found in our 20 years experience but it is very soon detected and corrected. It is a matter of selection and supervision as it is at the hospital itself.

Many of our patients are in homes where they have lived for a number of years. It is their home, they are a part of it and they would not wish to return to the hospital. Caretakers are made to feel that they are a part of our official organization and that certain standards must be maintained. They are invited on occasion to the hospital that they may learn the proper standards and for a general discussion of all problems relating to their work. Selection of the family caretakers is very much the same as the selection of employees for the institution itself. Best results can be obtained only by careful choosing.

Our experience at this hospital after conducting a family-care department for 20 years has been such that we believe the advantages to be:

1. To the caretaker:

    It provides a certain and dependable income although small.

    It provides occupation and company.

    It provides a home market for home products.

    It provides the taxpayer the opportunity of keeping and supporting his home.

    It makes less the taxpayer's burden for the support of hospitals.

2. To the hospital:

    It means a lessened need of building and equipment in proportion to the number of patients placed in family care.

    It allows the staff physicians more time for the study of the more acute and recoverable cases.

    The weekly per capita cost of family-care maintenance compared with that of the hospital is less.

3. To the patient:

    It means enjoyment of home life and freedom from the hospital.

    It offers a real opportunity for readjustment and possible eventual return to full community life.

First and finally, however, is the question, what is best under all the circumstances for the patient. Many patients do not need daily hospital care. They need a certain supervision which home might furnish if home were possible. If no home exists or is not suitable, then family care provides for many an escape from hospital existence to that of home life.

Family care, however, to be successful and worthwhile must be very carefully planned, properly supervised and safeguarded and allowed time for a natural and healthy growth. Lacking an intelligent backing, or carried on without careful supervision, it cannot be for the best interest of patients and will, therefore, most assuredly fail.

CHAPTER III

Experiences with Family Care at Newark State School

BY CHARLES L. VAUX, M. D.,

SUPERINTENDENT, NEWARK STATE SCHOOL, NEWARK, N. Y.

Newark State School began the use of boarding homes over four and a half years ago and now (1936) has a total of 103 mentally deficient patients residing in them. Lack of funds has prevented greater expansion but the project has gone far enough to make us feel that many more patients could be placed to advantage were sufficient funds available. Our first venture was with children of school age. I mention this here only to say that because of this experience we were encouraged to start three years ago a community modeled more or less closely on the familiar one at Gheel, Belgium. In fact, we have three different groups of family-care patients distinct as to type, placement and objective. They will be described in order under the titles we have found convenient to use in conducting them, namely: Family Care, Community; Family Care, Individual; Family Care, School.

FAMILY CARE, COMMUNITY

For our small community we chose the village of Walworth, N. Y., for many reasons which still hold good. A pleasant rural village of 300 people, it is located back in the country, several miles from the railroad and the main highways. The patients can walk the roads unendangered by traffic. Situated within 17 miles of Newark State School, it is accessible at all times in emergency and for frequent visits of supervision. Small farms and large gardens assure abundant food supply. Up to the year previous to beginning this experiment, orphan children from Rochester were boarded with many families so that the idea of boarding homes was not unfamiliar. The fact that it once was an academy town is said to assure a superior class of residents. The absence of industries makes improbable any future change that would affect our settlement.

The first patients were placed in January, 1933. By September of that year we had placed 32 in 14 homes. By January 1, 1936, the numbers in the community had increased to 80. Some patients live in the village, others on nearby farms. Patients were placed only with going families; that is, the family must not require the board money for their own support. The standard rate is $4 per week, which is not enough to provide for a patient in any place run as a regular boarding house. It is thought, however, that one or two extra mouths can easily be filled on a farm well stocked with food products of its own raising. The regular succession of dollars from this home-made market can be found very acceptable in a rural district where real money is usually so scarce. One or two to a family is thought most desirable. In most of the homes we placed two so that they could be company for each other and because their guardians felt that the second one would be no more trouble. We feel that in larger numbers the patients will not be absorbed into the family life to the degree that we would wish. Selection of the homes was made with the advice of two people from the village, the health officer and a practical nurse, both of whom were life residents there. Applications were numerous and many were rejected upon their advice. Whenever a home was recommended a written report of the home investigation containing a description of the home and the family was brought to the clinical director. This report followed the pattern that has been in use for years in investigating homes for parole cases, as shown in the following report of the first home contacted at Walworth.

BOARDING HOME INVESTIGATION

January 6, 1933.

Mrs. M. C.,
Walworth, N. Y.
Recommended by : Dr. E. E. E.

Home: The home is located in the center of the village. The house is large and pleasant and the lawn is spacious. The rooms consist of a hall, living room, dining room, kitchen, bedrooms, billiard room and bathroom. The girls' room is located at the front of the house on the south side, is a very pleasant room and very comfortably furnished. All modern improvements. The town of Walworth is about 17 miles from the school and about

Family Care, Community—Monthly Party at the Community Center at Walworth, N. Y.

Home for Patients at Walworth, N. Y.

7¼ miles from the main highway north of Palmyra. The road is a good country road. Walworth is a town of about 300 inhabitants, with two churches, a Baptist and a Methodist, three grocery stores, one of which is a grocery and drygoods combined, a high school and a grange hall.

Family: Mr. and Mrs. C. are in their late forties. They are very refined people and are highly recommended by Dr. E.   There are two daughters, aged 15 and 16 years, and an aunt of Mrs. C. makes her home with them. She is 83 years of age, and pays $10 per week for her board.

Religion: Protestant.

January 9, 1933: R. D. and M. N. were taken to Mrs. C.'s home this date. Board paid—$4 per week.

S. T. B.
Assistant Social Worker.

Selection of patients is made by the clinical director and takes into account what might be described as the accumulation of institutional dead wood. Patients who do nothing, and for whom nothing special needs to be done, are only in the way. If they can but sit, they might just as well do their sitting elsewhere to make room for those who can benefit by the training or medical care that the institution provides. Our patients are selected for this reason regardless of the degree of intelligence, so that the intelligence quotient of family-care cases has the wide range of 19 to 84. The average intelligence quotient is 50, half the patients rating as morons; the other half, imbeciles. Those in the high range, as might be expected, have something else the matter with them. One is blind, two have paralysis agitans; one is epileptic; one a cripple, and more than one partly psychotic.

The blind woman quickly learned to find her way about the small house, whereas the large institution building offered more difficulty. The epileptic had no convulsions until her new people had become acquainted with her. By that time, they had become attached to her and did not want to let her go, but gladly carried out directions for diet and medication. One woman who had episodes of depression, with a sulky period of several days duration, has had no spells for the three years she has been out. The patients with the tremors do not feel so conspicuous in a small house as in a large institution. The chronological ages range from 33 to 65 years. The older patients were the ones first placed. Some of these patients had been in the institution for 20 years, and were considered to have settled into most rigid and routine habits. It was surprising that even such cases rapidly made the adaptation to their new life and quickly made themselves at home in their new surroundings. Life in a family group is normal for human beings, and, with all living expenses provided for, life in a rural family is simple and natural and really makes few demands on the ability to adapt. Our patients have entered into the life of the family and almost invariably become part of it. They fit into the picture and look no different than the middle-aged aunt or sister found in so many homes.

The guardian was always given to understand that the patient's board was paid, and that she was under no compulsion to work for it or to earn her own way, but that idleness was not a natural state and the patient should be taught to interest herself in little tasks about the house and grounds for her own welfare. We thus find patients peeling potatoes, setting the table and occupying themselves in small ways as though they had always been a part of the household. The cooperation of the guardian is, of course, necessary to this happy state and we have invariably received it. One of our guardians who had many misgivings and was a long time in deciding to take patients, soon found she could turn over the entire care of her three-year-old daughter to one of the patients. The other one helped her around the house, but especially endeared herself by her banter with the woman's husband which kept him always in good humor. Now this woman would be most reluctant to part with her patients and treats them most kindly. In another home without any suggestion being made the guardian moved her patients downstairs when winter approached, as she thought they would be warmer in a room opening off the living room which was heated by the parlor stove. In the majority of the homes, patients sit down at the table to eat with the family. In all homes patients are regarded as human beings just like members of the family. This is favored by their living in such close proximity where the personal element is accentuated. There is nothing to develop the attitude of a nurse to her case, and no one has taught them the attitude of an attendant or keeper to a group of inmates. It has not been necessary to re-arrange patients in more than a few homes. The guardians develop such a personal liking for them, that they do not like to exchange no matter what trouble they might cause. One patient was annoyed by a small child, but adjusted all right in another home. Another adjusted satisfactorily when moved away from her patient companion. Another did no better after a change and had to be returned. Some were returned on account of illness, some for other reasons, and some for failure to adjust. These were promptly replaced by others who did adjust, and I wish to emphasize that the return of these patients had no appreciable effect upon our ultimate success. There has been no haste or hurry in securing homes. Placements were made one at a time fitting each individual to a home, which was a surer way than by attempting to place large numbers in a short time.

One of our social workers handles all of the work of the community, in addition to her regular duties. There is an advantage in her familiarity with the country and people, due to her having always lived in this district. Then, many of the problems met with were not new to her. The School has nearly 600 patients on parole at home, or in em-

ployment, or in colony houses in various towns
from which they go out for employment. Homes
and places of employment are continually being
investigated and hardly a day goes by that the patients are not returned or sent out to new places.
These patients in colonies or on parole in employment must be capable of earning the standard rate
of $3.50 per week, and so are not of the same class
as those selected for boarding homes, but the work
of judging the calibre of employees, of helping in
the adjustment of the patient, and of supervising
the patients' living conditions and welfare are
much the same, so that this experience is invalu-
able for family care. The social worker visits
every home once a month, but may visit a home
several days in succession after placing its first
patient, and calls at the community three or four
times a month. There is no question but what the
superintendent who has boarding homes should be
alert to all the dangers that threaten. Yet, I may
say that we cannot name them from our own experience. Most of the things we dreaded never
happened. The social worker gave to each new
guardian the instructions as to the proper care of
her patients customarily given to those taking girls
on parole, and any matters not understood were
corrected on her next visit. The necessity for
proper supervision was always stressed. A very
important addition to the supervision is afforded
in such a small village by the fact that every one is

known to every one else. As more and more families become guardians, it becomes the interest of more and more villagers to have their village recognized as a safe shelter for the patients. Of serious accidents, there have been none. There have been no escapes as there could be little motive at attempt to escape. The patients feel they have been placed on parole, many of them after having long given up any hope of such good luck. They are anxious to show that trust in them has not been misplaced, but most of all they are more comfortable than they have ever been before in their lives. Neglect has never been seen. Rather, the patients gain weight as they greatly enjoy home cooking after years of institution meals. There are no strict regulations as to food. What the family eats is good enough, but patients must receive that. By means of a small portable scales which the social worker always carries in her car, she can weigh anyone she suspects of getting too little to eat. During the severe weather patients were always found comfortably seated about the kitchen stove with members of the family in normal farmhouse style. Our own contribution, an issue of double blankets to every patient, no doubt helped at bed time. All patients have appeared clean and well cared for whenever visited. Exploitation is a bugbear to many. Our experience with parole cases is that employers are more apt to be too lenient and that in a small community some other employer

will be jealous enough to report most infringe-
ments of any kind. With adequate supervision
and quick action against offenders, it does not
seem that exploitation can be carried very far. Indeed, our experience has been rather in the other
direction. Passing over the many little gifts and
birthday parties to something of more moment, I
would cite the measures taken when any illness develops. Then specially cooked dishes are brought
to the bed, homely measures like hot mustard
foot baths are given or hot water bags are applied.
Simple medications are purchased at the local drug
store without thought of reimbursement. The family's whole concern is to relieve the pain, break up
the cold or alleviate the distress, and nothing is
too much trouble in the attempt to accomplish
this.

The small community affords good opportunities
for social life. All patients have the freedom of
their own premises. They go unattended on er-
rands to the village and to visit in each others'
homes. Hospitality is not lacking and they often
chat with each other over a cup of tea or a dish of
fruit. Some of them come to the village from a
considerable distance and it was thought they
should have some place to rest other than the post-
office steps. This was afforded when we established the community center. We contracted with
our first guardian whose residence was centrally
located to operate a community center in her home

and in addition to its use as a social center arranged that it should serve as a center for social service, nursing care, a depot for clothing and supplies and for occupational therapy materials. She agreed to the following regulations for the center:

RULES FOR COMMUNITY CENTER

1. A large warm room provided which has easy access outside so that all of the community cases may feel free to come and go for social intercourse and recreation. Adjoining this room, or in it, there should be at least two beds which should at all times be in readiness to receive any emergency sick cases or patients left at the room over night.

2. The day room should be provided with books, magazines, pictures, games, a radio and piano. Everything except the piano, will be furnished by the institution.

3. The one in charge should act in the capacity of nurse, looking after feet, hair, etc., of the neighborhood inmates and should keep weight charts (which will be furnished) on each case monthly. Corns and callouses should receive attention every three weeks or more often if necessary. Hair should be trimmed once monthly.

4. In the event that a patient becomes ill, she may be brought to the rooms where she can receive first aid and minor treatments, or she may require bed care for a few days and a record of temperature, pulse and respiration kept.

5. A patient may be left at the rooms if her boarding mother is obliged to go away for the day. Patients should not be left alone in their boarding places throughout the day.

6. The one in charge should endeavor to make the girls feel welcome and assist them in entertaining themselves.

7. Our occupational therapy director provides various forms of suitable occupation for those visiting the rooms.

8. The rooms are to be used as general headquarters where articles for the different girls may be left and clothing fitted, etc.

9. The one in charge should keep the social worker informed at all times of the various happenings and follow her advice in regard to general care, etc.

A supply of cathartics and some simple remedies are at hand at the center, but when a physician's services are required the local health officer is called and paid his regular rate. The occupational therapist visits all homes and lays out the projects, but depends upon the center to replenish supplies. There is greater need for this than was expected. It seems that patients once content to sit in idleness have been stimulated to the point where they complain if they have nothing to do. The occupational therapist arranges the monthly parties at which there is always a good attendance, besides which patients are accustomed to drop in any hour of day for the social facilities of the center. The nurse owning the house accepted $50 per month, the pay of an attendant, to cover her services and the use of the rooms thus engaged.

The attitude of the community toward us has been favorable. When patients were first placed one native asked our resident nurse what she was trying to do to the village, turn it over to "nuts." There are few evidences of such an attitude at present. Patients are welcomed at church and at entertainments; in fact, the admission rate is cut to fit the 25 or 50 cents per month they are given for spending money. Those who have been refused patients blame the nurse for not recommending them, but their being disgruntled seems to do us no harm. Just how many will ultimately apply for patients we cannot judge, but applications continue to come in. The general feeling among the villagers is good and any attitude of suspicion and distrust that may have existed has changed since they have seen the patients going about the village unobtrusively and have personally observed that they are not crazy.

We consider that the community has an outstanding advantage over any other type of placement, in that the experience will be accumulative. Careful selection of patients is obligatory in the beginning of a project like this. As the residents of the community become accustomed to having patients about, we feel that it is reasonable to expect not only that the individual guardians will become more willing to accept worse patients, but that there will be less looking askance at a patient of any kind. This is said to account for the success at Gheel where family care has been carried on through succeeding generations for several centuries, those now caring for patients having been familiar with their presence throughout their childhood. While we cannot hope to approach this in degree for a long, long time, nevertheless, those who are familiar with the small compact community at Walworth feel that this factor is already beginning to operate to our great advantage. It may be that such a long acquaintance with the project is not essential. Moreover, the effect of bringing approximately $20,000 yearly into the village is undoubtedly favorable.

Family Care, Individual

Entirely aside from our community placements, we would like to place a patient whenever we find a good home for her no matter where that home may be, because we believe that the most important thing is to get the right kind of guardian. It is borne in mind that the social opportunities of the community are not available for these isolated cases. Patients can be chosen who either would not respond to these advantages, if available, or on the other hand those who are able to use the social life of the locality in which they find themselves. Instead of a fixed rate, as in the community a sliding scale will be used. The highest rate will be paid for an idle patient in a city or where high prices prevail; lower rates in rural sections or for a patient with a little earning capacity, until we come down to nothing for one who can earn his own keep. Patients of this latter class are all we can afford so far. Of these, we have 7, 3 male and 4 female, widely scattered in separate homes. Such cases might be called "paroles," but as our paroles have to earn the standard wage no such patients were placed heretofore. It has long been customary for some counties to allow almshouse residents to go out to work for some family who could give them board and keep. This does not seem different from what we are doing and being able to add a little board money ought to make it easier to accomplish.

FAMILY CARE, SCHOOL

Family care, school, is in some ways different. Primarily its object is therapeutic rather than economic, but the procedure itself is simple. A child of school age, despite her commitment, is placed in a foster home in a village where there is a special class school and given another chance to grow up outside instead of being confined in the institution. Welfare agencies have boarded out children in a similar way for many years. Starting over four years ago, we are now carrying 16 children, 3 male

Two Patients with Their Foster Mother in Winter at Their Home at
Walworth, N. Y.

Family Care, School, First Home Established by Newark State School

and 13 female, in family care. They are in 9 homes in 6 nearby villages and attend 8 different public schools. The patients' ages range from 5 to 15 years, the average age on admission being 10. Their intelligence quotients range from 54 to 85—average 62.4. Many of them are enrolled in local scout troops, but a long story of these children's activities may be condensed by saying that they are not materially different from those of any other children. For their board we pay five or six dollars per week, as they live downtown where city prices prevail. We give them each 25 cents per week for spending money to teach them thrift and the use of money. In addition, we buy their clothing.

Already, we note favorable results. Manner, bearing and conduct have generally improved, and our children mingle naturally with their fellows in work and play. Four years ago, our 4 children were all in special class. Of our 16 today, strange to say, only 3 are in special class while all the others are making their way in regular grades. We are careful not to make the mistake of placing them too high, and do not mind if their grade is two or three years below that for their chronological age. It is striking that three children were ambitious enough to climb out of special class and gain regular grades. Of course, the matter of promotion is out of our hands and is made by the public school authorities without reference to our opinion. Our particular shining light is a girl, moron, who, starting in special class, is now progressing satisfactorily in the eighth grade at 16 years. Last year she was moved to another village to live with a fine family who have her interests at heart. They will continue her in school until it gets beyond her capacity and have plans to make her future both bright and secure.

Another of the first group was returned to her parents' home when she became 18 years of age to take a position at housework and in caring for children. For the past year and a half this girl in the high-grade imbecile class has been self-supporting.

Two brothers, aged 7 and 11 years, both morons, were returned to their home in Rochester on our representation to the agency by which they were committed, that for two years they had lived a normal life in the community and had made their promotions in regular grades in the public schools.

It is thought that the success of these children does not necessarily prove that they should not have been committed. No, rather it shows that when given a chance, under conditions as nearly ideal as could be devised, including the active support of a psychiatric social worker, they were able to adjust, while their histories show that they were unable to combat the handicaps of bad environment, poor parentage, physical disorder or malnutrition, and inadequate school facilities, from one or all of which they had suffered. Dr. Green-acre, psychiatrist, states that even the normal child brought up in an institution shows the effects of repressive discipline and tends to become stand-ardized, and that the department of welfare of Westchester County prefers to subsidize a child in its own home or to pay board for it in a substi-tute home, rather than commit it to the best of modern institutions. Yet the normal child can better overcome this handicap than the slowly ad-justing mental defective, separated throughout his formative years from the very experiences of liv-ing most necessary to his survival. We consider this important. What is done at this time affects the entire future of the child, and may determine whether he will be confined for life or otherwise.

We have other promising candidates selected for trial whom we expect to place when means be-come available.

SUMMARY OF PLACEMENTS

So far, the number of patients mentioned shows the maximum at any one time, but during the whole time numbers were returned for various rea-sons and replaced by others, so we have had many more in family care than so far shown—or a total of 165. Noting in each case the reasons for their removal from the boarding home, we find there were not many who failed to adjust.

Of the 124 in family care, community, 12 were sent to their respective county homes; 3 were transferred to family care, individual; 12 were returned to us because of illness or injury; 4 were returned to their State hospitals, 2 of these as unsuitable and 2 to go to their own family care; 3 were returned upon their own request, while 10 were returned as unadjusted.

Of the 18 in family care, individual, 2 were sent to county homes; 1 was sent to family care, community; 1 was sent to an employment colony; 3 were not needed longer by their employers; 2 were returned for illness and injury, while 2 did not adjust.

Of the 23 in family care, school, 3 were paroled to their parents; 1 was repatriated; 1 was returned because the home was unsatisfactory, while 2 were returned for misconduct.

FINANCING

Family care is financed by the State but only to a degree that limits any institution to approximately 100 patients. The legislative budget allowed, effective July 1, 1935, a yearly allotment of $20,000 for each hospital and school in the State Department of Mental Hygiene for the board of patients at a rate not to exceed $4 per week. Previous to that time we used the accumulated earnings of patients who had also received the privilege of living outside the institution but through another plan, that of the employment colony. These colony funds are used to make up the additional one or two dollars to cover the higher rate of board necessary for school children and to take care of all incidentals, as the budget provides for board only. We are glad to acknowledge that our neighbor, the Syracuse State School, helped us out on several occasions with cash donations when the drain on our own funds became too heavy.

In any new venture it seems justifiable to question if there might not be concealed costs which, if figured in, would wipe out the estimated savings. The figures submitted are for the six months period commencing July 1, 1935. They cover the actual amount spent as shown by our records, together with some estimates necessary to make a fair apportionment for this short period and to enable us to strike an average for the variations in numbers for different times. We have not attempted to compute the value of the time spent by the clinical director or the social worker. They have had an increase of duties without any increase in salary. Presumably, they rearranged their time so as to take care of that. Neither have we attempted to give the costs of transporting patients or social worker which, while unquestionably a required expense, is difficult to determine exactly.

FAMILY CARE—COMMUNITY

Board at $4.00 per week	$7,864 20
Spending money	167 92
Food for parties	5 07
Footwear	24 50
Repairs to shoes	90
Clothing, extra	35 11
Clothing, institutional	371 25
Blankets	92 50
Medical service	74 50
Drugs	1 23
Incidentals	14 50
Rental of hall for parties	6 00
Wages, resident attendant	324 00
	$8,981 68
Weekly per capita based on average of 75	4.56

FAMILY CARE—SCHOOL

Board at $6.00 per week	$2,239 47
Spending money	115 44
Footwear	84 30
Repairs to footwear	5 20
Clothing	479 82
Haircutting	13 80
Dental services	8 50
Medical services	113 90
Optical services	20 00
Incidentals, ice, gas and electricity at vacation colony, cleaning clothes, toothpaste, lunches for children on trip to Rochester and tickets to see doll house, etc.	57 74
Rental of vacation cottage	25 00
School supplies	36 76
	$3,199 93
Weekly per capita based on average of 14	8 57

FAMILY CARE—INDIVIDUAL

This includes 7 cases for whom no board is paid. The employer usually provides clothing and from 50 cents to $2. per week for spending money. We would take care of any bill for emergency medical services, etc., but so far have had little call for any extras.

For these children nothing is supplied by the institution. Even the clothing worn when leaving the institution is part of a new outfit purchased in the village. The high figure is considered justified by the expected economic results. For each case there is the all-time saving in institution space and the prospect that the expenditures need be made for only a few years. Comparing this with the cost of life-long institutional residence the ultimate saving does not require computation in pennies.

The combined weekly per capita cost of the two groups, community and school, is $5.21. If we add the third group, individual, which is just as directly a part and product of our family-care movement, we have $4.82. Combining only the last two groups gives us the figure for adults as $4.17. Thus all the figures are below the per capita for the institution—$5.95.

CONCLUSIONS

The foregoing experience with family care has demonstrated among other things:

1. That at least 100 mentally-defective patients can be comfortably housed and properly cared for in boarding homes.

2. That they can enjoy a happier and more normal kind of life with more liberty.

3. That the majority of families will take a greater personal interest in the welfare of the patient than their contract requires.

4. That the pursuit of a deliberate and conservative policy in making placements will do much to avert dangerous or even unpleasant incidents.

5. That many patients will improve and some sufficiently to raise their economic status.

6. That for placing adults the community affords many advantages.

7. That schools in neighboring villages will accept our younger patients without question.

8. That our confidence will be respected and no child stigmatized in school or village.

9. That many children of school age will attain a good social adaptation.

10. That the average per capita cost is less than for institutional residence.

11. That vastly greater savings are brought about in two ways:

(1) By relieving the State of the cost of maintenance of the patient for the remainder of his lifetime.

This occurs: (a) when patients acquire ability to support themselves, and results from training in school, or from experience gained in the community boarding home. (b) when patients are returned to the committing agencies: County commissioners, societies, relatives and friends can be induced to accept the patients they sent to us because we are able to present definite evidence that institutional residence is not required.

(2) By obviating construction costs which are said to double the actual costs of maintenance. Instead of erecting new institutional buildings to accommodate patients, we are making use of houses already built.

CHAPTER IV

Experiences with Family Care of Psychiatric Cases

BY HARRY A. LABURT, M. D.,
DIRECTOR OF CLINICAL PSYCHIATRY, HARLEM VALLEY STATE
HOSPITAL, WINGDALE, N. Y.

As differences of opinion exist as to what constitutes family care, a clear explanation of the term as here used should first be made. If a patient is able to make his own way in the community and adjust with the aid of an occasional psychiatric consultation, or is in the custody of his own family or relatives, he may rightfully be termed a regularly paroled patient. On the other hand, if a patient no longer needs active institutional treatment but needs psychiatric help and guidance indefinitely and is placed in the custody of a family, not his own, he may be regarded as being in "family care." With this broad interpretation of the term the family-care group would include convalescent patients as well as chronic types in which little or no improvement can be expected. If it is restricted to just the chronic deteriorated types who are placed in private homes and for whom the State pays maintenance, the term would seem inappropriate. The terms, "boarding care," "farm care" or "nursing care" would be more descriptive, as that is just where the patients would be, in boarding houses, farm houses or nursing homes.

Neither should the patients' ability or inability to earn some sort of an income affect the classification, as many patients both psychiatric and non-psychiatric can earn a modest income during convalescence.

Many objections to family care have been offered, such as, "the patients would be exploited, neglected; they would be a danger in the community; they would be unwelcome; it would not be to their best interests; it would be impossible to supervise them," and many others. Obviously, the project could easily become lost if all objections to it, both real and imaginary, were to be removed before it could be started.

Convinced that family care is feasible, it was decided to inaugurate it at the Harlem Valley State Hospital and meet obstacles as they arose. An active campaign was outlined and the plan was discussed with local health officers. Lectures and talks were given before social worker groups, parent-teachers associations, nurses organizations, granges, and other social agencies. These groups were given a general description of the plan and its aims and were informed as to the large number of patients that could be paroled into the custody of families in the communities. The opportunities afforded to carry out altruistic and humanitarian pursuits and the benefits to be derived by both patients and families were also explained.

The reaction to the plan was varied. Many persons were enthusiastic, others were unconvinced and hesitant, others skeptical and in some its conception was disappointingly garbled. A politician tried to capitalize the plan by telling his constituents, "If you want to get pay for taking care of patients, see me and I'll fix it for you." A county agent was openly antagonistic, and in a meeting of a health committee said, "Don't accept patients for four dollars a week and they will have to pay more."

As applications for patients were not received as rapidly as it was hoped, it was decided to have the patients "sell" themselves. Arrangements were made with a few of the better patients to work for maintenance only in two or three families in "key" communities, no one else to know for a time that they were patients. These patients behaved well, worked hard, and served as an example for later placements. Applications for patients naturally followed. Instead of offering patient help and paying for it, a salary and maintenance was asked for the better type of patients; only maintenance for the mediocre, and the four dollars a week allowance was reserved for those who could render little or no service. The "drive" was continued and the social service department made additional, desirable contacts.

Up to March, 1936, 36 males and 39 females, a total of 75 patients, were placed. Of this number, 12 men and 8 women were returned for various

A Patient in His New Position as a Farm Hand

A Patient and Her New Home

reasons, or improved to such an extent that they were discharged, leaving a total of 55; 24 men and 31 women. As to type, they may be divided into the following groups:

1. Chronic patients, in whom little or no recovery can be expected. They may be regarded as requiring mere custodial care. Three males and eight females, a total of 11 patients, are listed in this category.

2. Convalescent patients, in whom recovery or rehabilitation may take place through family care. Thirty-three males and 31 females, a total of 64 patients are listed in this group.

As to financial arrangements and expense they may be divided as follows:

A. Those who earn wages and maintenance.

B. Those who earn their maintenance only.

C. Those whose relatives bear the expense of family care.

D. Those for whom the State pays a weekly allowance.

Every placement is regarded as an individual problem and conditions are arranged to meet the patient's particular needs. No hard and fast rules are laid down other than the usual requirements for physical comforts and proper segregation as to sex. No home where there is distinct financial need is accepted. Each patient is to have a separate bedroom. However, two beds for patients in one room would be approved. The members of the family, their ages, personalities, location of home, reason for requesting a patient, type of work to be performed, etc., are considered together with the patient's age, sex, type, characteristics, personality, former occupation, aptitudes and adaptability. If everything is found to be satisfactory, the financial arrangements are made. One patient in a family is preferable, two acceptable and in only two instances have three been placed in a family. Two of the patients have been returned from one family and the three in the other family, who live on a large estate, still remain.

To dispel any semblance of coercion or compulsion, the patients are made to understand clearly before they leave the hospital that they do not have to stay with the family unless they so desire. The families are assured that they may return the patient for any reason whatsoever.

Foster families should thoroughly understand the patients and their disorders and assume a proper attitude toward them. An inquisitive woman unknowingly caused the return of a patient by investigating the patient's family background and discussing it with her. This discussion aroused painful conflicts and the patient became disturbed. Caretakers are informed of the patient's special traits or peculiarities, if any, and instructed in a general way as to the best methods of management.

Before placement, it is necessary to resolve any

transference that may exist between a patient and any member of the hospital personnel. The following cases are illustrative: Lily T. was placed as domestic in the home of a physician. After three weeks she insisted on returning to the hospital to be near her ward physician. It was unknown at the time of placement that a transference existed. Bertha H. had to be returned from three placements before her transference to a staff physician could be completely resolved.

Patients' remunerations are commensurate with their abilities and services. They range from $5 per month and maintenance to $150 per month and maintenance. The social worker secured the latter salary for a male patient placed as manager of a country club. This patient has not been listed in family care but through it a satisfactory arrangement has been made for him. He had been an able advertising man capable of earning a large annual income. Because of personality problems and conflicts he sought recourse to alcohol to supply a deeply-seated psychological need and to mitigate the problems of adjustment. After several months treatment he improved and as he was an ex-college athlete with a good physique and an engaging personality, the position was obtained for him. He carried on well for the remainder of the summer, under the guidance of the owner, a kindly old banker. Whether it was due to an exacerbation of his old conflicts or the conviviality of the patrons,

or both, it is not definitely known but he became ill
again and lost his position. He was next placed as
advertising manager for a private sanitarium at a
much lower salary but with free weekly consultation with the attending psychiatrist. He is now
getting along very well and making a satisfactory
adjustment.

The average salary obtained for male patients
has been $15 to $30 per month and maintenance
and for females, $10 to $20 per month and maintenance. This is the largest group, consisting of 25
men and 24 women, a total of 49 patients, of which
17 men and 22 women still remain.

A smaller group consisting of 9 men and 4
women, a total of 13 patients, of which 5 men and
1 woman remain, were placed in "free homes" receiving maintenance only for whatever services
they could render. In some instances the hospital
supplies their clothing.

Two men and 3 women with private means, of
whom 2 men and 2 women remain, and 7 women (4
remaining) whose expense of maintenance is borne
by their families, were placed. These afford a
higher rate of pay averaging about $10 a week,
which may be used to augment incomes of caretakers who accept "free patients" and those paying lesser amounts. Experience has taught that
these placements must be handled with caution.
Relatives to whom the plan was broached cooper-
ated well, in fact, one too well. He stated that he

couldn't possibly pay more than $10 per week for
the maintenance of his sister, a former grand
opera star. She was accordingly placed with a
nearby family. After a time she became rather
tempestuous and was returned. She again improved and the brother, without the knowledge of
the hospital authorities, went back to the caretaker
to rearrange for her placement. She, remember-
ing the patient's temperament and his reluctance
to pay more than $10 a week and desiring to rid
herself of him, said she couldn't possibly take his
sister back for less than $20 a week. He, much to
her surprise, instantly accepted the offer and she
found herself with the patient in her custody
again. Unfortunately for the hospital, however,
the caretaker later went about the neighborhood
telling that she was getting $20 a week for the pa-
tient's care and now others are asking for a like
amount. It appears best, therefore, not to let one
caretaker know what any other is paid.

Of the patients whose maintenance is paid by
the State, three have been placed and only two remain. They were placed in order to demonstrate
that the plan could be applied to this type also.
As it is desired to place the better patients in more
advantageous positions, and incidentally to the
State's advantage, efforts have not been directed
toward the dependent group to any great extent.
However, as demands for the other groups dimin-
ish more attention will be paid this one.

6

One placement usually suffices for the majority of patients. Occasionally, even when all factors seem to be satisfactory, a placement fails and repeated efforts may be necessary.

Our 75 patients required 112 placements. Of this number, 13 men required 31 placements and 13 women required 32, a total of 63 placements. Roughly, about one-third needed more than one placement. Efforts were abandoned in the case of one man after four trials. However, in the case of a young dementia præcox patient, Rose D., who has a poor family background, a happy situation was brought about after four trials. She was first placed as a maid in a physician's home. The social standards there, apparently, were too high. She went home without permission and was subsequently returned. Next, she was placed as a laundress near her home. Family distractions were too trying and she was again returned. Her next position was that of domestic in a family with three grown children. Competition for attention in this family was too keen, she became upset again and had to be returned. After improvement she was next placed with an elderly couple of about her own social stratum. This couple's deceased daughter would have been about the patient's age if she had lived and, therefore, they welcomed the patient with open arms. Her adjustment now seems to be very satisfactory as the family treat her as a daughter and take her wherever they go.

They supply her with that long-needed parental solicitude and guidance and she in turn fills a long-
existing void in their family life. As the arrangement in the family is new, a social worker calls
about every two weeks to aid in their mutual understanding and adjustment.

Two male and three female patients required
four placements each. Another male patient required three placements; 10 male and 10 female
patients required two placements each, and the rest
one.

No difficulty has been experienced in placing patients on account of their nationality or race. The
group placed includes two male and four female
negroes. Occasionally an application is received
requesting a patient of a certain nationality. An
attempt is made to meet the caretaker's wishes but
no objections are offered if one is not available
and a patient of different nationality is substi-
tuted.

Patients are visited from time to time, some
more often than others, by a member of the social
service department, or by a physician if medical
consultation is needed. The patients are encouraged to write as often as they wish to register any
complaint or dissatisfaction.

Four men and one woman left homes of their
caretakers without consent. Two of the men were
returned; the woman returned to the home of a
former employer and as she was getting along

well, was permitted to remain. Word was received from one of the men in Arizona and it is hoped that the other one, a nomad, arrived safely in China.

Men patients have been placed in 14 different occupations, of which "farm hand" is the largest group, consisting of 13 patients; 4 are listed as handymen and 3 as PWA laborers. Country club manager, short order cook, gardener, farm manager, farmers, dairymen, waiter, seaman, carpenter, gas station attendant and porter claim one or two each.

Occupations among women patients are not so varied. Twenty are listed as maid, 2 as housekeeper and one each as nursemaid, pantry girl, clerk, leather worker and beautician.

In order to meet the demands for farm workers, a class under the direction of the hospital farmer has been established. Patients are taught milking and the general rudiments of farming.

A domestic arts class under the direction of the dietician has also been started to teach women patients the general principles of housekeeping and dining room service. As male patients can be placed as restaurant workers and waiters these occupations will be included in the instruction given relating to dining room service.

Patients are receiving instruction in the various institutional beauty parlors. One "graduate" has already been placed and is doing well.

A female patient appeared to have made good progress and was placed in the home of a family in a desirable community. Within a few days she became difficult to manage and almost ruined the contact. In order to forestall any such recurrence, a "trial home" or "half-way house" has been established in the private home of an experienced hospital supervisor. Patients of doubtful adaptability will be tried in this home for a week or two before placement.

Naturally, an outlook has been maintained for "exploitation" or overworking of patients. Our observations have not revealed any form of misuse or neglect. On the contrary many instances of kindness and sympathy toward patients could be cited. The following are examples:

Charlotte R., an old arteriosclerotic patient, and Josephine S., an old depressed patient, ingratiated themselves so deeply in the hearts of their caretakers that the latter hired a housekeeper to look after the patients when the caretakers took a European trip. Josephine was given custody of her small insurance policies and she derives great pleasure in going to town each month to forward her 17-cent premium to the insurance company.

William R., a simple paretic, was so well liked by his former caretaker that the latter refused to sell his gas station unless the buyer took "Bill" also. Bill is now just as well liked by the second caretaker. Bill takes as much pride in the station as the owner himself.

The following excerpt from a letter in regard to a patient, Carl V., indicates one caretaker's attitude:

"Gentlemen:

A week ago I called you up telling you that Carl wanted to go back to the hospital. He was kind of tired and thought he did not do enough. The heavy snow we had bothered him in getting around. I know I got tired stamping around in it and it is so much worse for him with his big feet. He is a greater worker and when he cannot do much he thinks he is not earning his living. I reasoned with him and got him to take it a little easier . . ."

As the patient refuses to use the family sitting room he is provided with a private one adjacent to his bedroom.

The caretakers of Annie S., a little old Scotch patient, were very fond of her. Annie went to church and the theater with them and wrote "this is the life." Annie, over 60, was placed in the home with Mary S., over 60 and Mary R., aged 19. Annie in her desire to be the center of attention played Mary against Mary and the both of them against the caretaker. The result was that both old ladies had to be returned. As a rule, it is best not to place old patients with young patients in the same household.

Placing patients in situations where social de-

A Patient Working in the Yard of His Foster Home

A Patient Sweeping the Porch of Her New Home

mands are light and occupations not too difficult has been most successful. Catherine F., a former private secretary, is very happy in her new position as housekeeper in a physician's home, in which she receives excellent supervision and is readjusting very well. Robert F., a former police officer, is contented in his position as waiter in a restaurant conducted by a retired attendant. May L., formerly a woman of means, is very gracious in her new position as housekeeper in a dentist's home.

Advancing them in the social scale has had its successes also. Elizabeth B. was an accomplished pianist with a well-known symphony orchestra but never associated with the right people. She was placed in a wholesome family group in a nearby city. She resumed her music and is now quite prominent in musical circles. Her brother states: "She has never been so well." The grand opera star, previously mentioned, is now getting along quite well and is taking part in community musicals. Her caretaker is well known in her community.

Families are pleased not only with services rendered by patients but also by companionship they contribute to the home.

Edward S., employed as a farm manager, converted the farm from a losing enterprise to a paying one, much to the satisfaction and profit of his caretaker.

John N. is doing exceptionally well as a handy-man in a private school. He proudly carries out the duties assigned to him.

A county attorney who employs Anna H., a young manic, writes that "she is the best maid they ever had." She is practically an adopted daughter of the family, plays and goes skating with the young children and assumes the rôle of "big sister" to them.

The caretakers of Rose D. said "they always wanted a daughter and now they have one."

The caretakers of Henry S., an old senile, are very grateful for his presence in their home as he keeps "grandpa" occupied at chess every day. They are now "buddies."

Through family care two male patients and one female patient improved to such an extent that they were restored to their families. Improvement in two men and two women enabled them to secure better positions with larger incomes.

A more wholesome attitude toward mental disease has been noted in the communities where patients are placed. Family care is responsible for the change.

Mrs. ——, a prominent woman in the community, bitterly opposed the coming of the hospital and later resented the presence of patients in her community. She was induced to accept a patient and later liked him so well that she asked for another to be placed on her son's farm.

Another caretaker said "It is the duty of the citizens to aid in the rehabilitation of patients. . . . " She is unusually competent and conscientious in supervising her patients.

Robert F., now a waiter, is always welcome in the local men's club whose membership includes the leading citizens of the community. They all display a wholesome interest and attitude toward patients.

Though new and in an experimental stage, our experience seems to indicate that family care is feasible. We believe that the project has possibilities of serving as a useful and humane method of supplementing hospital treatment. Our objective is to re-establish patients on a self-supporting basis. By wise placement in families, patients, both chronic and convalescent, are enabled to resume life in a more natural setting, with more freedom than could be possible in a State hospital. Family placement provides a home for those who have none or whose homes are unsuitable. It often aids in quicker rehabilitation by offering the patient a more normal step between hospital and social readjustment. It also provides an outlet for community altruism and improves the economic status and security of the caretakers.

Doubtless, new obstacles will be encountered and mistakes made but with gathering of experience, revisions and modifications may reduce these to a minimum.

The plan is more economical for the State, at least that has been our experience. In times of depression or prosperity, no difficulty is anticipated in placing patients.

In the future, "social centers" with an employee in charge could be established in various communities if the project becomes sufficiently extended to warrant them. These would widen its scope, facilitate its administration and possibly reduce costs.

More important than all else, patients in family care are happier, more contented and natural. They look more human and act more human. Anyone who has visited them and talked to them will attest the fact. Patients quickly adapt to their new life and when given a choice to return to the hospital with its comfortable beds, steam heat, showers and with no responsibility for cooking and laundering, or to stay in the home, be it ever so humble, they invariably choose the latter.

The establishment of a project such as this is beyond the ability of any one person. It requires the skill and earnest cooperation of an entire organization. It was made possible at Harlem Valley State Hospital only through the impetus given it by the State Commissioner of Mental Hygiene at the time it was inaugurated in the department, and by the hearty and enthusiastic cooperation of the entire hospital staff.

CHAPTER V

Nursing Homes for Mental Patients*

BY PHILIP SMITH, M. D.,

MEDICAL INSPECTOR, NEW YORK STATE DEPARTMENT OF
MENTAL HYGIENE

The subject which I am calling to your attention
brings up the consideration of private care and
treatment for mental patients from a different aspect than that which is in existence at the present
time. The number of patients under private care
is small as compared with those in the institutions
supported by public funds. This is mainly due to
the fact that either the patient himself or his relatives are unable to meet the expense which is en-
tailed by private care. Still, in many instances,
strong efforts are made by the relatives to obtain
private care, although it works considerable hard-
ship on their resources.

In a survey made by the National Committee
for Mental Hygiene in 1930, reports were received
from about 180 private institutions for mental patients in the United States. About 100 are under
a license which is granted by the state in which
the institution is situated, but almost the same
number are functioning without a license. In some
of the smaller states, practically all of the institutions are unlicensed, and even in those states which
which require a license, some of the institutions

*Originally read at Quarterly Conference at Marcy State Hospital, Sep-
tember 12, 1933.

which are recorded are taking mental patients and operating without a license.

In the State of New York at the present time, 1936, 30 institutions for psychotic, and 12 institutions for mental defective patients have been licensed by the Department of Mental Hygiene. Definite regulations have been formulated in regard to them and the law is specific in its statements. Each institution for psychotic patients must be in charge of a qualified licensed physician who has had at least two years experience in a psychiatric hospital. There also shall be in charge of the nursing service a nurse who is a graduate of a training school in a psychiatric hospital or, if not of that kind of hospital, shall have had an adequate experience in the nursing care of psychiatric patients.

In private institutions for mental defectives, the individual in charge must present evidence of experience in the care of mental defectives which is satisfactory to the department.

The location for the institution, its construction and internal arrangement, equipment, capacity, fire protection, water supply, sewage disposal, are other factors which are taken into consideration. If, after inspection by a representative from the department, and usually also by one from the office of the State Architect, everything is satisfactory and all unfavorable features have either been removed or corrected, license is issued for a year with the privilege of renewal at the end of that time.

Visits of inspection are made at regular intervals, and reports are made in regard to general or special matters, as well as granting interviews to all new admissions.

Although the law is specific in stating that no mental patient shall receive care in an institution except one which is licensed, instances occur, from time to time, where complaints are made that psychotic patients are receiving care in other places. The number of places of this nature to which attention has been directed is not very large, but there is a tendency for more of them to arise in the future. At the present time, 16 of this class of institution have been placed on record by the medical inspector and regular visits are made in order to ascertain if any patients have been admitted who are psychotic and should be committed under the Mental Hygiene Law. In several instances, regularly qualified physicians have sent their patients to these institutions. In addition to regular visits which are made to these established unlicensed institutions, visits are made to others in regard to which complaints have been made that they are harboring psychotic patients. On making these visits there often is considerable protest from the owners, and the statement is made that there are many others which are conducted quietly and never attract attention.

The place usually is owned and conducted by women who call themselves "practical nurses"; only in a few cases have regularly-trained nurses been found.

The patients usually are of the senile type, with variable degrees of mental and physical enfeeblement. In some of them it is of mild degree, but in others it is profound dementia with scattered delusions and transitory hallucinations. Occasionally there are patients with frank psychotic symptoms and others again show only physical debility or paralyses.

The usual procedure which has been followed is to order the removal of psychotic patients either to a State or a regularly licensed institution. When the mental condition of the patient does not warrant commitment, although there may be some mental symptoms, no interference or action has been taken.

The attention which is given to patients in these unlicensed places is mainly of a custodial nature; they are kept clean; have regular hours of sleep; are fed at regular intervals and kept out of the way of any harm or difficulty. Nothing of a therapeutic or constructive nature is done, as in most cases only a vegetative existence is led.

Compliance with the recommendation and order to remove psychotic patients is not always followed and in several instances legal procedures have been started or followed out. In one case in greater New York court proceedings were brought against an unlicensed physician who had two places in which he was harboring patients. Four of these patients were definitely psychotic, either having been in a State hospital or being still on parole. The case was dismissed after a brief hearing. In the second instance, the owner of the place was a nurse who was not registered. Here, again, the charge was not sustained, although two patients under care were definitely psychotic. Both defendants had clever counsel who raised the objection that the defendants did not know at the time that the patients were psychotic. The court sustained the objection and rendered a verdict of acquittal. In another case, although a patient in an unlicensed institution was considered insane by the medical inspector, two outside practitioners took an opposite view, and in view of the possibilities of a similar result occurring if legal action were taken, the opinion of the two physicians was accepted.

Failure to obtain a conviction acts as a drawback and a source of embarrassment to the medical inspector, when such instances may be cited in support of places harboring psychotic patients in other localities. In several instances, the colonies in connection with the State schools have been mentioned. The establishment of boarding-out homes such as have been started at Walworth and have been functioning for some time in the state of Massachusetts, will no doubt be cited in the future in justification of the maintenance of these unlicensed places. The assertion has been made that the difference between a colony and an unlicensed place is that the former is in charge of attendants who are under the supervision and direction of the institution, while an unlicensed place is functioning under independent management.

The establishment of colonies has been carried out in Europe over a considerable period of years. The colony of Gheel under Dr. Sano is so well known that only a brief mention need to be made. About 3,000 patients have been placed in a district which is about 17 hectares in extent; usually only one, and no more than two, patients are placed in a family at rates of compensation varying from the equivalent of six to eight dollars a month in the lower walks of society to about one hundred dollars a month in the higher grades of families and establishments. The patients fall into the arteriosclerotic, senile and other quiet deteriorated types.

At Oetweil near Zürich there is a colony of several hundred patients of this same type; many of the patients are sent from the Burghölzli hospital and are supported at a moderate cost from public and charitable funds. This same hospital also has about 300 patients who are in placement in families in outlying districts at a moderate rate of compensation. A further example of this boarding-out system of patients was met in connection with the hospital at Buch, near Berlin.   Here again there is a regular out-patient service under the direction of a physician from the hospital. He has about 300 patients under his supervision who have been placed in families in the surrounding country for an average of 60 marks, or about the equivalent of $15 a month.

In England, an institution called the "Nursing Home" has been in existence for years, the first one, called the Metropolitan Home, having been established in 1840. The Convalescent Home Association came into existence in October, 1905, and some regulations were followed out in the establishment of homes for the care of patients recovering from acute physical conditions. These homes were established rather easily and practically the only requirement was a permit from the landlord who owned the property. There was no control over the owner or the establishment, and there followed the usual result, namely complaints of abuse and ill treatment. These finally came to the attention of the Minister of Health and the British Medical Association, and resulted in the passage of the Mental Treatment Act in July, 1930. The law became operative on January 1, 1931, and was acclaimed as one of the great constructive measures in regard to the care of mental patients. Many of the provisions of the act are similar to those of our Mental Hygiene Law, but one of the striking features was that patients could be admitted on a voluntary status to both public and private institutions and nursing homes without the usual process of certification.

A board of control, consisting of five senior commissioners, had supervision and control over these institutions and was empowered to enact rules and regulations and to make regular visits of inspection. One of these commissioners is the chairman, one is a woman, a third is a legal commissioner who has had a definite period during which he has been a registered barrister; two are medical commissioners who, for a period of at least five years, have been registered practitioners.

The members of this board are on duty at headquarters and make only special visits of inspection to the institutions, the bulk of visitations being performed by subordinate commissioners. The total number of these shall be such as is fixed by the Minister of Health with the consent of the treasury. Eleven of these subordinate commissioners were appointed in 1931 by the board of senior commissioners with the approval of the Minister of Health.

After the passage of the Mental Treatment Act, the board of control exercised statutory power for the approval of any hospital, nursing home or place desiring to take voluntary patients, temporary patients or patients receiving single care. Every existing nursing home was subjected to a minute and rigorous inspection and each head of

such a home was served with a list of requirements which had to be made for its continuance.
Some of the existing homes could not meet these
requirements in regard to structural alterations,
equipment and segregation of patients, and had to
be discontinued by their owners.

In making application for a license for such a
home, instructions published in pamphlet form
were called to the attention of the applicant. It
also was advised to ascertain if there were any unfavorable features or if the establishment of such
a home was detrimental to the neighborhood. As
far as possible, it was the aim to have such homes
located in particular sections of cities or villages.

Three main essentials were required:

1. Adequate means of escape in case of fire.

2. Adequate equipment and satisfactory interior arrangement in regard to space, segregation,
etc.

3. That there should be a qualified resident
nurse in charge unless there was a qualified resident medical practitioner.

Approval of the license was given for a year,
with the privilege of renewal at the end of that
time.

The capacity of these nursing homes ranged
from about 10 in the smaller to 420 in the largest;
the former are usually in outlying districts and the
larger homes are in the cities. These latter show
a good internal arrangement with adequate nurs-

ing and surgical equipment and affiliation with medical practitioners. Also, boards of visitors who see patients who are admitted. In the smaller homes where there is no board, the visitation of patients is made by two visitors who are connected with some of the larger homes in that vicinity.

Ordinary private houses are used for the smaller homes but are not considered ideal, and the trend in the future is toward the erection of specially constructed and equipped buildings.

The class of patients admitted to these homes were those suffering from mild mental disorders, seniles, chronic invalids, alcoholics, and in some of them maternity cases were taken although the home was classed as a mental one. Others, in their printed announcements, stated that mild mental, nervous and epileptic patients were received. One home, called Barnsley Hall, received private patients from one of the mental hospitals. There were other homes which limited their admissions to drug and inebriety or neurasthenic, senile, chronic and rest-cure patients.

The number of trained and untrained personnel in the home depends on the type of patient admitted. In an ordinary home one night attendant or nurse for each six patients was the usual number. The administration of the institution is subject to the local regulations which are made either by the nurse or physician in charge.

The compensation paid for the care of patients in these homes is variable; in the outlying, provincial districts patients are received for from 1½ to 3 guineas, or approximately $7 to $15 a week. In other homes the charge is from the equivalent of $25 to $160 a week. The drug and inebriety cases can obtain treatment for about $30 a week.

All cases admitted to mental hospitals, licensed institutions and homes are reported to the board of control. The report of this board shows that on January 1, 1931, the number of insane in England and Wales was 144,161; in the private institutions there were 14,404. However, the number of certified patients in the latter institutions who were psychotic was only 1,106; the remaining number, therefore, were mostly of the class which I have previously mentioned, namely, senile, chronic, etc. Since the admissions are not limited to those that are psychotic, another feature of the report is that these cases who are in single care of an individual also are reported, and of these there were 91 women and 258 men, a total of 358. The classes of patients admitted to these mental homes are similar in many respects to those which I have mentioned in connection with the unlicensed institutions which are found in our State. These places are not of the same standard as the present-day English nursing homes, but the standards which exist have been set up only since the Mental Treatment Act was passed in 1930. At that time, abuses had arisen which made inspection and control a necessity. Evidently the English nursing home has passed through various stages and only rather recently have the present standards been adopted.

There is an aversion in the minds of many people toward the hospital or institution supported by public funds, and when it becomes necessary to remove a troublesome old person from the family circle the unlicensed institution is sought by those whose means do not permit care in a regularly licensed institution. The compensation usually is not high, ranging from $12 to $20 a week as an average rate. There also is the further consideration that the place has only a small number of inmates and more individual care and attention is given than in a public institution; further, there are no restrictions, and rules are elastic and flexible.

Although these unlicensed places are not of a high standard, they apparently are fulfilling a need for people to have their relatives receive some form of private care at an expense which they can afford. Necessary care and attention to ordinary comforts is all such patients require. If these patients did not receive care in the unlicensed places, they would eventually gravitate and be admitted to a State institution.

It is a question where these deteriorated cases properly belong. Unless there are demonstrable psychotic symptoms, they are classed as dotards and are not retained in a state hospital, but transferred to the almshouse.

Apparently it would be of economic value to the State if some measures could be devised whereby cases of this nature could be under some form of private care commensurate with the resources of the family.

The unlicensed institutions are, in a measure, fulfilling a need but nothing has been done in regard to exercising any control or supervision over them. In the isolated instances, visits are made by the medical inspector and in the 16 which I have previously mentioned, fairly frequent visits are made, but only to ascertain if any committable psychotic patients have been admitted. Otherwise no attention is paid to the care, attention or management. The general care of the patients is left to the judgment of the individual in charge.

These places are rather easily established and often there is no one aware of their existence or nature except those who are directly interested. They are usually kept secret and any outside intrusion is either prevented or resented.

Some recognition and supervision should be exercised, and certain standards should be adopted for the control of the places which are in existence and for any which may be established in the future.

Places of this nature should operate under a permit and be registered. The class of patient admissible to such an institution should be limited to mild mental cases, seniles, deteriorated quiet cases, chronics and neurasthenics, but no active or acute conditions.

The persons in charge of the institutions now in existence might be continued, but, unless the qualifications are very satisfactory, a qualified nurse should be added, or one sufficiently experienced. Any future applications should meet the three main essentials, a qualified nurse in charge, adequate equipment and arrangement in the interior for segregation and exit in case of fire; also sufficiency of personnel. A physician should be on call in emergency and periodical visits should be made by him at least once a month. Reports of the movement of patients should be forwarded monthly as in the case of other licensed institutions.

In conclusion, it might be stated that the establishment and recognition of this form of institution will eliminate the unlicensed institutions which are in existence, some of them already under supervision and others coming to the front from time to time.

It will enable people of moderate means to provide for their old and infirm patients at a low rate of compensation. Further, it will be of economic value to the State to have these patients under some form of moderate private care and prevent them from reaching the public institutions.

CHAPTER VI

Practical Considerations Relating to Family Care of Mental Patients*

BY HORATIO M. POLLOCK

That mentally diseased and mentally defective patients of certain types may be placed safely and advantageously in the care of private families has been amply demonstrated both in this country and abroad. Of the countries of Europe, Belgium, Holland, Germany, Sweden, Switzerland, France, Scotland and Hungary are using family care to a considerable extent. In this country, Massachusetts is the only state that has had long experience with family care. New York has made a beginning and several other states are giving the matter serious consideration.

The advisability of the introduction or of the further use of family care in any state must naturally be determined by public sentiment and other conditions existing at the time. If it is decided to introduce family care in any state, attention at the outset must be given to certain practical considerations. These include:

1. The system of family care to be adopted.
2. The selection of patients.
3. The selection of families.
4. Rates to be paid for care of patients.

*Read at meeting of American Psychiatric Association in Washington, D. C., May 16, 1935.

5. Supervision and treatment of patients in family care.

6. Extent of use of family care.

These matters will be discussed in order:

1. *The System of Family Care to Be Adopted.* The outstanding systems at the present time are: a. The community system, of which the Gheel system is the best known example; b. The Scottish system of placing patients in isolated families; c. The German system of maintaining patients in their own homes or in the homes of strangers under the immediate oversight of a central hospital. This system is probably in most extensive use at Erlangen, near Nuremburg, Germany. Variations of these systems are in use in other countries.

If great use is to be made of family care, I believe a system somewhat like that in use in Gheel possesses many advantages over the other systems. Assuming it is decided to establish community family care in this country, the system would naturally be conducted by state hospitals or state schools. Community centers would be located in rural villages within easy distance of the state institution. The community house would serve as an intermediate station between the state institution and the families receiving patients. Patients would go from the state institution to the community center and from there to their family home. If it became necessary to return a patient placed in family care, he would be sent by the family to the community center and then either to another family or back to the institution. The community house would be the headquarters of the physician, social worker, occupational therapist and others who would supervise the patients placed in family care. The house would provide a meeting place for patients, and would be equipped to provide emergency aid to patients when necessary. The beginnings of a community group such as I have in mind may be seen at Walworth, New York, where nearly 100 mentally-defective patients have been placed in family care by the Newark State School.* A community center has been established at a convenient location in the village, and the system is working to the satisfaction of everybody concerned.

The plan of placement whereby patients are put in family care in widely-separated farm or village homes could be used with safety if great care in placement were exercised, but the system would not easily lend itself to large-scale placement and would not afford proper advantages to the patients in the way of recreation and social life. Adequate supervision in such a system would be extremely difficult.

The system of paying families to care for relatives in their own homes, which is being used to a considerable extent in Germany, would probably not be satisfactory in this country. Great care

*See Chapter III.

should be exercised in avoiding conditions that would give rise to the continuation of neuroses such as those which have been found so troublesome in veterans' hospitals. When a patient becomes mentally ill, his own home as a rule does not constitute a suitable environment for him. The environmental conditions giving rise to his conflicts would be continually before him and in many cases the persons charged with his care would be closely identified with his difficulties. It might be possible in some instances to aid an indigent family when a member of the family is returned to the home on parole but the matter is one which would have to be handled with prudence.

The home of a mentally-defective patient, as a rule, does not have proper facilities for his care and training. If either of the patient's parents were defective, it would be poor policy to pay them for the care of their child.

2. *The Selection of Patients for Family Care.* Good judgment must be exercised in selecting patients for family care. In state hospitals, until a system of family care is well established, it probably would be best to place only tractable patients beyond middle age. These, in the state hospitals, would include quiet schizophrenic, chronic manic-depressive, and other patients who have established a more or less settled routine and are not trouble-makers.

In the schools for mental defectives certain types of children may be selected for family care in addition to both men and women beyond middle age.

In instituting a system of family care it is highly important that the patients placed out should not be disturbing factors in the community. A public sentiment favorable to the system should be built up. This cannot be done if too heavy burdens are placed at the start on the families receiving patients.

In the mentally-diseased group, types not suitable for family care would include the following:

a. Patients that need constant medical or nursing attention.

b. Patients suffering with mild or acute mental disorders who are likely to make prompt recovery.

c. Patients that are disturbed or suicidal.

d. Patients that are quarrelsome, contentious or have pronounced delusions of persecution.

e. Patients with marked erotic tendencies.

f. Patients that have severe convulsions.

g. Patients that are suffering with infectious or contagious disease.

Mental defectives not suitable for family care would include all idiots; most low-grade imbeciles; most patients with marked physical defects or deformities; patients that have a tendency to run or wander away; patients unclean in their habits or who cannot be trusted to keep themselves properly clothed.

After excluding all cases clearly not adapted for family care, a large number of suitable cases will remain, and from these, selection must be made to fit the home which is to receive the patient. If, at the time of placement, the family and the patient are both satisfied, the success of the placement is highly probable. On the other hand, if the patient enters the home of a dissatisfied family, or if the patient himself is displeased with the home to which he is assigned, the placement is likely to be a failure.

3. *The Selection of Families to Receive Patients.* In beginning a community system of family care it is a common experience that good families hesitate to apply for patients, and families that do apply are likely to be found unsuitable. After a family-care community becomes well established and well understood, applications from suitable families are frequently received and placement becomes easier.

The requisites of a home for the placement of patients would include:

a. A comfortable house in which a satisfactory room for one or two patients could be provided without crowding the family.

b. A garden plot on which vegetables and flowers could be raised.

c. Proper heating arrangements so that patients would be kept comfortable in winter.

d. Wholesome family life.

e. A friendly attitude toward the patient on the part of all members of the household.

Stable well-established families of the middle class would be most likely to cooperate successfully in this undertaking. After a time it might be possible for the placing institution to give a course of instruction to those desiring to become guardians of patients.

4. *Rates to Be Paid for Care of Patients.* As patients are less desirable in the home than normal boarders, the maximum rate paid for the care of patients should be somewhat higher than the customary boarding rate in the community. On the other hand, it is probable that the maximum rate for patients should not exceed the institution cost of maintenance exclusive of housing. A low rate should be paid for patients who can assist materially in housework or in farm or garden work, while a much higher rate should be paid for those who can do no work and need considerable personal supervision. The maximum rate for indigent patients in Massachusetts is $4.50 per week, and in New York, $4 per week.* If the patient is not indigent, the rate may be fixed directly by his committee and the family receiving him.

*In 1936.

In instituting a system of family care, a state should not make the maximum rate too low. A low rate would mean a low standard of care and general dissatisfaction. If a state can place patients in family care and thereby save housing costs the gain in the course of years would be enormous. To seek more might endanger the whole project.

5. *Supervision and Treatment of Patients Placed in Family Care.* A reasonable degree of supervision should be given patients placed in family care but the matter can be easily overdone. Perfection in conduct and adjustment cannot be expected of either patients or guardians. The supervising and social workers should visit patients at irregular intervals and should be available to render assistance in case of accident or emergency. An occupational therapist should have general supervision of the activities of family-care patients, other than their home duties. Projects suitable to the capacity and environment of the several patients should be provided and each patient should be given adequate instruction. To produce the best results the interest of guardians in patients' projects should be developed.

The physician in general charge of family-care patients should endeavor to safeguard the health of his charges by cooperation with guardians in arranging hygienic living conditions and providing a proper routine of activities for each patient.

Whenever practicable, patients with serious illnesses should be brought back to the state institution for treatment.

6. *Extent of Use of Family Care.* There are great possibilities for family care of mental patients in rural villages of this country and comparatively small opportunities for such care in large cities. If the community system of family care proves as successful here as in Gheel, many large community groups could be established. The Scottish system or Massachusetts system could also be widely used. I believe, however, that the community system is better adapted to large scale placement.

In bringing this discussion of practical considerations to a close, I would call your attention to a serious conflict that is developing in our social and economic life; namely, the conflict between ideals and economic ability. We wish to maintain the highest standards in all our social and public enterprises. We build great palaces for state and Federal government offices; we erect magnificent schools, colleges, hospitals, prisons and welfare institutions. We furnish all of these with the most elaborate and costly equipment. We construct expensive highways throughout the length and breadth of the land. We build and scrap great battleships for which we have no use. We do all these and many other similar things while our countryside is decaying and our cities are on the

8

verge of bankruptcy. Probably 90 per cent of oui citizens are either dependent or in marginal circumstances. There is serious question whether the ideal institutional system we have set up can be enlarged and maintained so as to provide for all patients needing treatment. It follows that there is imperative demand for any practical economies in the care of mental patients that can be effected without reduction of standards.

PART II. FAMILY CARE IN EUROPE

CHAPTER VII

The Lesson at Gheel

BY EDGAR A. DOLL, PH. D.,

DIRECTOR OF RESEARCH, THE TRAINING SCHOOL AT VINELAND,

NEW JERSEY

Gheel is a Belgian town of 3,000 families, situated about 40 miles east of Antwerp and easily reached by train from that city or from Brussels. Its recent "rediscovery" by psychiatrists and public welfare officials has been the result of an increasing number of pilgrimages to the *Colonie de l'État belge pour le traitement familial des affections mentales*. The uniformly favorable reports brought back by students of this enterprise, and the effectual publications of the superintendent of the Colonie, Dr. Frederick B. Sano, have created a wide interest in this family method of treating mental patients. The idea seems equally valid for other types of defective, delinquent, and dependent persons.

This Colonie is a national institution under the supervision of the Department of Justice of Belgium which provides for the supervision, care and treatment of approximately 3,000 mental patients (insane, epileptic, and feebleminded) in private families. The central Colonie is a clearing center for about 100 patients in temporary residence for purposes of observation, diagnosis and classification. New patients remain at this center a few days or several weeks until suitable arrangements for their placement in private homes in the town can be made. To this central institution patients also may be returned for shorter or longer periods of further observation, diagnostic review, reclassification, special custodial care, treatment, or training. The central institution also provides accommodations and educational facilities for a limited number of juvenile patients.

The remainder of the patients, which is to say almost all of the 3,000, are boarded out in the town of Gheel and its surrounding parishes. The standard practice is to place two patients of the same sex and of about the same age and type in a family. Of course, the families are carefully investigated, or their status is known from association with the Colonie for many generations. Placement is made with due regard for the social and cultural level of the patient and of the foster family, and also with regard to the mutual occupational interests of patient and family. Approximately 1,500 families, or nearly half of all those in Gheel, thus receive patients and provide for their needs. Close contact is maintained with the central institution through visitation by members of the hospital staff, and the arrangements are so informal that continual contact is maintained with the cen-

Main Hospital Group at Gheel

Administration Buildings, Colony Gheel

tral institution for the immediate transfer of patients to and from institution and family.

This arrangement is so satisfactory to the inhabitants of Gheel that at the present time about 400 vacant rooms are available for patients, and about 125 new families per year make application for the reception of patients. Patients are not placed in families where intoxicating liquors are dispensed commercially nor where suitable occupation, recreation, supervision, and sympathetic understanding cannot be provided.

The central institution is located just outside the town, two or three miles from the railroad station. It occupies an extensive farm site and resembles the typical small mental hospital in a rural situation. This central plant provides hospital facilities, administrative offices and staff, about 100 beds for patients, a school for children, a commissary and store, and the usual accessories of an institution whose major occupational activity is farming supplemented by simple crafts and trades. There are no walls or fences; patients come and go between the institution and their family homes with the utmost freedom. The patients also have practically unrestricted freedom within the town and live as ordinary members of private families, subject only to a few simple restrictions which are necessary for their welfare. Most of the patients are generally known, or are easily recognized, by the normal residents and are treated with sympathy, kindness, and respect. All types of families, from retired bankers to industrious cobblers, receive patients. This source of income is not unwelcome to these thrifty families, supplementing as it does their rather meager earnings as farmers, craftsmen, or tradesmen. But over and above this economic interest, there prevails an obvious sympathy, and a sense of beneficent social responsibility which is the principal guarantee of the success of the plan.

The Gheel program has a long and interesting history. Toward the end of the sixth century (according to legend) Dymphne, the daughter of an Irish king, sought refuge at Gheel to escape the unwelcome obsessive attentions of her father, who sought an incestuous union with her. She and her confessor escaped to Belgium, but were pursued by the king, whose soldiers murdered the priest and beheaded the daughter. Her tomb subsequently became a shrine at which the mentally afflicted prayed to Sainte Dymphne, and many miraculous cures added to her renown. As the possessed and the persecuted continued to come from far and near to visit the shrine for refuge or for cure, the obscure village of Gheel gradually became a well-known refuge or asylum for the mentally defective and disordered.

As time went on and public accommodations were overtaxed, the hospitality of the homes of the town was extended to those unfortunates. Subsequently, a *Ziekenkamer,* or hospital, was established under church auspices. As the work grew, it became subject to local governmental regulation, and in 1852 these semi-religious and semi-communal facilities became the nucleus of a state colony for the care of mental patients. Ten years later an *Infirmerie* was built providing for 60 patients; this was soon enlarged to a capacity of 100 patients. The whole is now operated as a modern mental hospital with a medical director in charge.

In recent years the Colonie has increased its provision for family care to the extent of 3,000 patients. During the past 60 years, approximately 25,000 patients have passed through the Colonie and the program now commands international attention by its extraordinary success. The movement of population is approximately 500 patients per year. Patients are received from all countries of the Christian world.

The majority of patients are naturally of Belgian residence. Indigent wards of the state are received at a rate of 8 Belgian francs per day.* State wards are also received from Holland at a rate of 12.5 francs per day, while private patients from Holland pay 25 francs and up. Private patients from Belgium and other countries are received at varying rates according to the family accommodations provided, the top rate being about 40 francs

"These rates were in effect in 1933 and may have changed since that time. The minimum rate paid to the foster family was then 600 francs per annum."

per day, or about 15,000 francs per year. It is a little difficult to translate these costs into American terms, both because of the fluctuation in the rate of exchange and of money values and because of the higher purchasing power of money abroad. With the Belgian franc at five cents, these rates would range from approximately $150 per year for Belgian state patients to a top rate of $750 per year for foreign private patients. The private rate is determined in large measure by the type of accommodations desired in the foster home and by the amount expended for clothing and extras. Fifteen per cent of the private rate goes to the central Colonie for medical and scientific provision. A relatively large percentage is retained by the Colonie for the overhead cost of state patients, whose total rates are much less than those of private patients. A patient's guardian may, within certain limits, select the foster home and arrange for the private rate, subject to the approval of the Colonie. In those instances the classification may be made in advance and the patient may be admitted directly to the private home or after only a few days residence at the central institution.

All types of mental patients are received. The majority of patients are psychotic or psychopathic, but some epileptic and feebleminded patients are also admitted. Violent patients whose condition may not prove amenable to family care, or might constitute a nuisance or a menace in the town, are referred to custodial institutions, or cared for at the central infirmary during the manic period. This means that only the more favorable type of patients is placed in families. But all the patients are socially irresponsible and most of them make excellent adjustments even though they may have been gravely disturbed, and even violent, at the time of placement. The attitude and experience of the foster families account largely for these successes for many of these families have participated in this program for generations, so that remarkably sympathetic and intelligent care is the rule. From one generation to the next a kind of tradition has been built up with such a definite degree of beneficent spirituality toward the idea that many families believe this work has divine inspiration and reward. This is reinforced by the Gallic attitude toward the mentally handicapped as the special concern of *le bon Dieu*. The children of these families, growing up as they do in association with the patients, are prepared to continue the work and of course the additional source of income is always a motive of some importance.

The program appears to be highly successful, for relatively few difficulties are encountered. There seems to be no evidence of fear, scandal, or violence. This is due, in part, to the close and sympathetic supervision of both family and central staff. Patients may be returned at a moment's notice to the central institution for custody, treatment, or readjustment. This is particularly important for the epileptic and episodic patients. A record is maintained in each family for each patient, and this casebook is subject to inspection by the medical staff without notice. Likewise, the patient may be visited without notice at any time. Both routine and special visits are made without formality. The patient is therefore always "on view" and the families are constantly on the alert to maintain good standing with the medical director of the Colonie. With an excess of families desiring patients, it is obvious that the families do all they can to hold their wards. There is naturally some element of disgrace or loss of community prestige in the event that the Colonie no longer approves a particular home. Contact and supervision between the family and the Colonie are simple and immediate, due to the proximity of the institution.

The occupations in which these patients are engaged reflect their immediate environment. Sometimes the placement is related to occupational aptitudes previously acquired at home or before the onset of the abnormal condition. Otherwise, occupational skills may be acquired in the new environment. These occupations naturally reflect the family situation in which the patient is placed. Nearly every family has its own garden or farm or domestic stock. The community has no large industrial organization, but does provide the usual ar-

A Typical New Home at Gheel

A Foster Family at Meal Time in Gheel

tisan and commercial pursuits common to the European country town, such as cobbler, baker, butcher, and merchant. Most of the patients act as helpers in the family and assist with the garden work or engage in the family occupation. Many of them achieve an astonishing degree of occupational success in spite of their mental handicaps.

For purposes of medical supervision the Colonie is divided into four sections, each in charge of a physician assisted by two nurses. These doctors and nurses continuously visit the patients in the families allotted to their section and are responsible to the medical director for the welfare and health of these patients. The physicians are not permitted to engage in private practice; as officials of the Department of Justice of which the Colonie is a subdivision, they devote their entire services to these patients. Each section is provided with a large bathhouse to which patients are periodically taken by the foster families.

Two official bodies supervise the work of the Colonie. One of these, a high commission, is composed of the governor of the province, the king's attorney, the district justice of the peace, the burgomaster, and the curé-dean. This commission supervises employee personnel, medical program, budget, material equipment, and the like. The second supervisory group is a permanent committee, composed of the local burgomaster, local judge, three members designated by the Minister of Justice, and the physicians of the Colonie. This committee has charge of placing indigent patients and those other patients whose boarding homes are not selected by their guardians. The permanent committee is concerned principally with the personal welfare and home conditions which surround the individual patients and in respect to which individual privileges or restraints may be exercised.

In addition to these supervisory bodies, the people of Gheel constantly exercise indirect control of the utmost importance, zealous as they are for the success of this work. With patients coming and going about the town, and with family conditions well known because of proximity, untoward events are readily controlled through public opinion. Thus the rules regarding the frequenting of taverns and the restrictions on the serving of intoxicating drinks are "sanctioned through community approval and enforced by the police." Incidentally, patients are not permitted away from their foster homes after dark.

The professional visitor at Gheel is received with gracious hospitality, not to say cordial enthusiasm. At the time of my own visit, Dr. Sano was busily engaged with a meeting of the high commission and also was entertaining a delegation of visitors from several different countries. I was nevertheless courteously showed about the central plant until Dr. Sano was free to see me. I shall not soon forget the buoyant, youthful enthusiasm with which he discussed his program. The warm personal elements in the administration of the program were reflected in his hearty "Bonjour" as we entered house after house from the central plant to the Cathedral of Ste. Dymphne. Whatever skepticism one might have at a distance is immediately removed by seeing these patients living normal, happy, useful lives as members of families who treat them as respected members of the family group, if not even as guests to whom some special deference is due. We saw patients at refreshment in taverns, conversing with townspeople in the streets, engaged as bakers' helpers, as clerks, as gardeners, as messengers; in short, in many useful, if relatively simple, occupations and activities. The freedom from any suggestion of restraint other than that watchfulness which parents exercise in varying degree according to the responsibilities of their children at different stages of development, was in sharp contrast with even the most intelligent and sympathetic care one sees in our best American hospitals.

The personal interest in the patient required by the very nature of family care obviously insured an immediate knowledge of each patient's habits and needs and an intimate acquaintance with his affairs which guaranteed that no patient was "lost" in the scheme. The very naturalness of the situation was its most powerful argument and one could readily envisage many American communities of like rural situation and communal cordiality in which similar programs could be promoted in this country, provided it were done with sufficient care and without undue haste. Indeed, such a community is now to be seen at Walworth, New York, where a family-care colony program for feeble-minded has been organized by Dr. Charles L. Vaux, superintendent of the Newark (N. Y.) State School, which is an American Gheel in miniature.

The advantages of the Gheel plan are immediately evident. There is, first of all, the almost entire saving of the cost of plant and equipment. This investment cost of buildings and grounds is usually ignored as part of the maintenance cost of institutionalized patients. It is generally estimated, however, that the overhead cost of plant and equipment is approximately equal to the annual maintenance cost. This item is therefore entirely saved except for the investment in the central infirmary and the overhead for the supervisory staff. In the typical American institution, where the average bed cost ranges from $2,000 to $4,000 per patient, the annual investment charge at five per cent would range from $100 to $200, exclusive of depreciation and replacement. Moreover, since the original cost of plant and equipment is frequently a serious bar to making adequate provision for large numbers of patients, it is readily seen that under the Gheel plan a small initial outlay for a central institution and staff provides the

immediate means for caring for many more patients than is possible under the typical congregate
hospital plan.

In actual practice, competent authorities estimate that the family care of state wards can be
provided at approximately half the institutional
cost, if the overhead for plant and equipment is included in the total. In addition to this financial
saving, or perhaps as a result of it, evidence shows
that under the Gheel plan approximately twice as
many patients can be cared for annually. The
Gheel plan, moreover, reduces public resistance to
providing the necessary funds, since the public has
a definite unwillingness to invest the initial large
sums necessary to provide bed space and other
services.

The advantages to the patient are many and obvious. The family or guardian of the mental patient is usually apprehensive regarding state institutional care in spite of the high standards
achieved by most state institutions today. There
is an inevitable loss of personal identity on the
part of the patient in large state institutions,
where the patient cannot receive that solicitous
personal attention which his relatives so earnestly
desire him to have. Life in a state institution is
inevitably regimented and standardized, with some
consequent loss of regard for the personal needs
or wishes of the patient. In the typical state hospital the patient loses much of his freedom that

need not be lost to him in family life, and much of his self-expression is sacrificed to the needs of mass care in the limited environment of the large institution. He is almost entirely cut off from association with relatives and friends and his emotional life is frequently inhibited just as his social activities are gravely restricted.

Because of these conditions, which obtain to greater or less degree in even the best hospitals, there is some negative therapeutic effect of the environment which is oppressive to the patient and which is particularly unfortunate for those patients to whom restraint, rather than controlled guidance, is a stimulus to excitability. To the mental patient, therefore, a state hospital has many inevitable aspects of a prison, with many of the abnormalities and restrictions of environment and associations that must result therefrom.

Can this idea which has been so successfully developed at Gheel be extended to the care of mental patients elsewhere? There are, of course, obvious hazards. A sympathetic and cooperative point of view must be built up with a public which has for many years accepted public institutional care as a traditional method of dealing with mental patients. Obviously the right communities must be found and the program established by slow stages of growth. No such program can be imposed as a complete project in a short time. Once established, the sympathetic public viewpoint must be safe-

Home of First Rank for Care of Patients at Gheel

Interior of a Villa for Patients of the Upper Class at Gheel

guarded by a careful selection of homes and careful selection of patients as well as by judicious correlation of patient and foster home.

Institutional authorities and public welfare officials cannot escape the criticism that may result from scandal or other misfortune on the part of patients committed to their care. This constant fear seriously limits the success of institutional programs which might otherwise more aggressively promote the social rehabilitation of their wards. It is therefore not surprising that institutional authorities hesitate to risk being held responsible for the possibility of failure on the part of patients who have been returned to the community. If 99 patients are discharged or paroled as improved or cured, the public returns but little praise to the institution, but if one patient is so unfortunate as to get into trouble, the fact of his having been a ward of this or that institution stirs up ill-considered criticism toward the institution that released him. It requires extraordinary courage for the institutional staff to release the 99 who might be successful, lest there be that one who might be unsuccessful. Until the public becomes more generous in its attitude towards mental patients who have been released, the institution can hardly be expected to risk its reputation for the sake of the individual patient when there is so much at stake. This is not to say that our public institutions are not conscientiously returning patients to the communities from which they came; we merely emphasize that to do so requires courage and imagination sufficient to overcome the fear of public censure.

This same fear of public criticism intimidates the medical superintendent or the public welfare official who sees in family care benefits that cannot be attained under institutional conditions. This is not because our institutions are not well managed, but rather because they cannot duplicate the conditions which obtain in a private home. To these superintendents, these officials, and this critical public, we may well call attention to the fact that the majority of all mental patients are now living in family care. Every mental patient has been cared for in his own family most of the time, if not all of the time, prior to his commitment, if indeed he is ever committed to an institution. Many thousands of mental patients are now being cared for in their own homes because of unwillingness on the part of the family to part with the patient for sentimental or other reasons. It has been estimated that, even in those states which provide the largest proportion of institutional facilities, less than 10 per cent of the feebleminded are cared for in institutions. In some states no provision is made, and in the majority, provision is made for less than five per cent of the feebleminded. Precise information regarding the number of committable epileptic and insane now living in their own homes as compared with the number living in public and private institutions is not available, but probably the majority of the committable epileptic and insane are not living in institutions but in their own private families.

Public officials need not, therefore, in fact assume that family care is impracticable when the majority of mental patients are now living in private homes. It is an unfortunate but unavoidable fact that a mental patient once committed to an institution acquires a stigma which inevitably haunts him if he should later be released, just as it haunts the institution if he should get into trouble after release. On the other hand, the patient's own family usually is not a suitable place for his care and usually entails upon the relatives a burden which is all too frequently a menace to their mental health and economic welfare. Moreover, mental patients now living in family care without the medical supervision that would be provided if such family care were available (as under the Gheel plan) seldom receive adequate professional treatment and guidance. Not until we can think of the institution as a general hospital rather than as an asylum can we look forward to the day when admission to a state institution can be something less than the life sentence that the idea of permanent custodial care so often means. Even when constructive programs of modern medical treatment are actively pursued there is a tendency to hold the patient such a length of time that institutional habits are established which work to the detriment of the patient if he is returned to his own family. A system of foster family care set up between the institution and the patient's own family offers certain benefits not to be lightly disregarded.

In all history the family has been the critical social unit. Family life is the core of community life and the pivot around which most social activity and personal conduct revolve. While the public institution is a simple and convenient way of caring for state wards *en masse,* even those now devoting their lives to this form of social welfare have recurrent misgivings as to the ultimate wisdom of the method. The days of the insane asylum have passed, but even the new mental hospital cannot provide the advantages to the patient which are inherent in family life.

On the other hand, it is well-known that the mental patient is frequently unadjusted in his own family because of those emotional fixations which are built up between the patient and his immediate family. These fixations result from the extreme solicitude of the family for the welfare of the patient and give rise to overprotection by the family which engenders unreasoning resentment in the patient. This emotional projection of the relative toward the patient creates a subjective attitude on the part of the relative which is contrary to the

Schoolhouse for Children Patients at Gheel

New Central Bathhouse at Gheel

best interest of the patient. The experiences at Gheel show that the foster family assumes an objective attitude toward the patient which is less protective or less obsessive that that of the patient's family, but is more solicitous and more personal than that of the public institution. The foster family frequently achieves a wholesome sublimation of its own emotional needs in caring for mental patients, by substituting these patients for other relatives who have either been denied them or lost. The Gheel plan provides for an adjustment of family to patient and of patient to family which all too frequently cannot be achieved when the patient's family must provide for him in the parental home.

In defense of the advantages of institutional care of mental patients over family care, it should be emphasized that the above argument loses much of its weight when applied to those institutions which provide aggressive, constructive programs of remedial treatment and training. Some of our leading state hospitals, such as the New Jersey State Hospital at Trenton, have promoted programs of medical treatment and occupational training which require institutional residence under hospital conditions. The same may be said of the treatment and training programs required for epileptic and feebleminded patients where intensive rehabilitation programs may require more or less continued institutional residence. In relation to such programs the plan of family care is most useful during the convalescent period before the patient is returned to his own family as sufficiently improved or cured to resume his former place in his own community or family circle. Institutional rather than family care is also more advantageous in the case of bed-ridden, senile, grossly deteriorated, chronically disturbed, and similar patients who cannot receive proper attention in a private home because of the practical difficulties of managing the patient.

It is not difficult to conceive that the Gheel plan might be extended to other types and degrees of dependent, defective, and delinquent classes. Thus the family care of the feebleminded should be a far simpler problem than that of the family care of the insane. The family care of the epileptic, however, might be relatively more difficult. Family care of the environmentally delinquent and of the blind, the deaf, and the crippled, and others who are mentally, physically, and socially handicapped, opens a vista of possibilities which requires imagination as well as courage. What has already been accomplished in America for normal dependent children by substituting foster family care for institutional care is only one encouraging example of what can be done.

While there are, and for many years will be, differences of opinion as to the merits of family care of the insane and other classes of dependents, it is significant that already this idea has received enthusiastic support by leading psychiatrists and several international conferences. The great social and therapeutic value of such care is well expressed in the second resolution of the International Congress for the Care of the Insane held at Antwerp, 1902, as follows:

"For a very large group of the insane, the family colony represents the most natural form of assistance, the most free, the best and the least expensive, and it moreover constitutes, for a large number of patients, an important therapeutic factor."

CHAPTER VIII

Family Care in Germany

BY HORATIO M. POLLOCK

The beginnings of family care of patients with mental disorders in Germany date back to the eighteenth century. As early as 1764, Dr. Engelken, a former army physician from Holland, placed patients, from his small private hospital in Rockwinkel near Bremen, in families in Ellen and other farming communities in the vicinity of the hospital. The placements were made at first without careful selection of patients and guardians and the care given patients was not well supervised. Family care, so inadequately begun, has continued in that region down to the present time. Marked improvements were instituted by St. Jugens Asyl in Bremen in 1878. More care was exercised in the selection of patients and guardians and patients placed in homes were given better medical supervision.

Other institutions report the year of introduction of family care, as follows: Goddelan, 1863; Berlin-Wittenau, 1886; Bunzlau, 1886; Richberg, 1869. Ten additional institutions began family care between 1890 and 1900, and 45 more from 1901 to 1914. From 1914 to 1936, war, inflation, poverty, and changes in government seriously interfered with the progressive development of family care. On the other hand, the lack of funds for the building of new hospitals has necessitated home or family care for many mental patients.

Family care in Germany has been greatly influenced by the wisdom and vision of Dr. Wilhelm Griesinger who died in 1867. Writing in the 60's, Griesinger expressed ideas concerning the care of the insane which were far in advance of the thought and practice of his day. His paper on "Institutions for the Insane and Their Future Development in Germany" was translated by Dr. Frank E. Smith and published in Volume LX of the American Journal of Insanity, which appeared in October, 1903. In this paper Griesinger set forth what he considered to be desirable provisions for the care of the insane in Germany. After discussing asylum and hospital care and psychiatric clinics, he took up the question of open-door care which he thought should always be closely associated with the "closed" asylum. He regarded with favor two types of open-door care, namely, care in agricultural colonies and care in private families. He discussed the latter with prophetic vision. The plan he developed is in the main the plan of family care as it exists in Germany today. We quote the following from Dr. Smith's translation:

"Generally speaking * * * there are to be found influences still more beneficial than those of the colonies. These are to be found * * * in the family care, which for a certain proportion of the insane is the right and only appropriate method. It offers, what the finest and best managed institution can never give, a full life among the sane, the return from an artificial or monotonous existence to a natural social atmosphere, the benefits of family life. Quiet, absolutely inoffensive patients, still receptive to the influences which belong to this kind of existence, who are not altogether estranged from life, and who are still capable of benefiting by the majority of the healthy forms, on the whole, females rather than males, are admirably adapted to this kind of open-door care and stand in urgent need of it. With such patients, more particularly, the family life can be begun. Gradually and almost imperceptibly it will take in all those who are not included in the categories of the permanent inhabitants of the closed institutions.

"The family system can be realized under two kinds of modifications: (a) In the case of a rural institution in the neighborhood of small villages or towns a certain number of patients can be entrusted as boarders to honest respectable farmers, artisans and the like, one or, at most, two patients to each house. The whole care, employment, nutrition and accommodation must be under the supervision of, but not actually provided for by, the institution. An inspector or assistant physician every day, or according to circumstances every second day, should visit all these houses. At first the patients, for half a day, twice every week, can come into the institution until caretaker and patient become well acquainted with one another. The patients should share in the work, meals and in fact in the whole family life of the caretakers. The latter, therefore, should be people of about the same station in life, of the same education and calling; the former tailor should be assigned, when possible, to a tailor, the farmer to a farmer. Of course, the assignment of the individual patients to appropriate families is part of the duty of the institution and should never be left to the relatives of the patient. The cost of board will be arranged with the family, some slight allowance being made for the work done by the patient.

"But it might be asked, how about the care of the patients? Can it ever be so good anywhere as in the closed institution with its airy sleeping apartments, its garden, its water supply, its three meals daily, at which is served excellent food prepared by means of the most modern and best kitchen arrangements? To this question there is but one answer. Ask the patients who are now under family care, but who were formerly in excellent closed asylums, whether they would like to go back. The well-being of man, i. e., the real personal recognition that it is well with him, depends but very little upon such things, but is largely a matter of feeling. He that is not fitted for the closed asylum and for whom it is not a matter of necessity, looks upon such a place as a prison house for the flesh-pots of which he never pines. And he is right."

One of the most successful of the early German experiments in family care was that made by Ferdinand Wahrendorff, director of a private institution for mental cases at Ilten in the province of Hannover. This highly-esteemed physician instituted a well-planned system of family care in connection with his institution in 1880. Beginning with four patients in three families, the system grew rapidly, until, at the death of Dr. Wahrendorff in 1898, it comprised 140 patients who were living in congenial homes in neighboring villages

So powerful was the influence of Wahrendorff and so far-reaching were the effects of his experiment that he has been named "The Father of Family Care in Germany."

The development of family care since the days of Griesinger and Wahrendorff has devolved almost entirely on the individual institutions. The director could keep all his patients within the walls of his hospital or could place part of them in family care. Patients placed out remained patients of the hospital and could be brought back or transferred to another family home at the will of the director. For this reason the family-care system of Germany became known as the annex system as distinguished from the "colony system" at Gheel, or the "dispersion" system of Scotland. At its best the family care of a German hospital is a supervised treatment procedure allied to occupational therapy and recreational therapy. For certain classes of patients, family care is a preliminary step toward parole or discharge; for other classes it may be simply an economical method of maintenance.

As would be expected, family care has had an uneven and irregular development in the several German states. From data collected by means of questionnaires sent to the hospitals for mental patients, Konrad Alt reported that there were 1,200 patients in family care in Germany in 1902 and 2,400 in 1906. Later data, resulting from a questionnaire, sent in October, 1927, by Dr. E. Bufe of Uchtspringe to 154 hospitals in Germany are presented in the tables given below.

CHANGES IN FAMILY CARE IN GERMANY FROM APRIL 1,
1909 TO OCTOBER 1, 1927*

April 1, of each year	Institutions conducting family care	Patients in family care
1909	49	2,502
1910	50	2,638
1911	54	2,791
1912	57	3,116
1913	59	3,392
1914	60	3,741
1915	65	3,815
1916	64	3,726
1917	63	3,371
1918	61	2,836
1919	62	2,514
1920	62	2,166
1921	58	1,902
1922	57	1,895
1923	55	1,646
1924	50	1,511
1925	51	1,793
1926	52	2,127
1927	54	2,554
October 1, 1927	58	2,816

It is seen that a notable increase in family-care
patients occurred during the years from 1909 to
1914. A decline, which set in during the World
War and continued during the inflation period,
reached its low point in 1924. The number of patients reported in family care in that year was
1,511. Following the stabilization of the mark, the
number again increased and had reached 2,816 on
October 1, 1927. Dr. Bufe found the distribution

*Psychiatrisch-Neurologische Wochenschrift for April 28, 1928, p. 176.

of family cases in the several German states on that date, as follows:

FAMILY CARE IN GERMANY ON OCTOBER 1, 1927

State	Institutions With family care	Institutions Without family care	Total patients	Patients in family care
Prussia	43	25	64,105	2,529
Anhalt	..	2	894	..
Baden	..	6	4,756	..
Bavaria	1	16	11,991	11
Brunswick	..	1	614	..
Bremen	1	..	897	174
Hamburg	..	2	3,589	..
Hesse	3	5	3,571	7
Lippe	..	1	423	..
Lubeck	..	1	349	..
Mecklenburg-Schwerin	..	2	948	..
Mecklenburg-Strelitz .	..	1	193	..
Oldenburg	..	3	630	..
Saxony	5	5	8,983	52
Thuringia	1	2	1,843	2
Wurtemberg	4	1	3,042	41
All Germany	58	73	106,828	2,816

Since these data appeared there have been noteworthy developments in family care in various parts of the Empire but definite data relating to its present status are not available. Dr. Bufe in discussing family care at the International Congress on Mental Hygiene in May, 1930, made the following statement:

"In Germany, foster-family care suffered considerably from the war and post-war periods, but

it is gaining now. Of 140 hospitals, 85 have foster-
family care, with about 4,300 boarding patients,
that is, about 4 per cent of the total number of
mental patients.''*

Noteworthy among the German hospitals conducting family care in 1927 was Hadamar Hospital in Hessen-Nassau which, with a total of 407
patients had 134 in family care. Wittenau Hospital in Berlin, with 2,239 patients, had 426 in
families. Bremen-Ellen Hospital in Bremen, one
of the first of the German hospitals to introduce
family care, was using such care for 174 of its 897
cases. Twelve of the German hospitals had over
100 patients in family care and three of these hospitals had more than 200.

The cost of maintaining patients in family care
varies considerably in the several German states;
also in the different hospitals of a single state.
Furthermore, the amount paid a family for the
care of a patient by any one hospital is not uniform but depends on the condition and working
ability of the patient. In 1927, the German hospitals were receiving from all sources for hospital
care an average daily allowance per patient of
3.20 marks. For the patients placed in family care
the hospitals paid foster families an average of
1.37 marks per capita per day. The payments for
single patients varied from 0 to 3 marks per day.
After making a liberal allowance for the expense
of supervision of family-care cases, it is seen that

*Proceedings of First International Congress on Mental Hygiene, page 393.

substantial saving results from family care. More-over, every patient placed in family care leaves a bed free in the institution for another patient.

A noteworthy variation from the usual method of placing patients in families in Germany is found at the Mainkofen hospital in lower Bavaria. This institution pays nothing to the family that takes a patient but expects that the work of the patient for the family will be adequate compensation for his room and board. Only one patient is placed in a family. He must have his own room and take his meals with the family. To supply the patient with pocket money and to keep him contented, the hospital pays the patient 75 pfennigs a day; a portion of this amount, however, is placed in a savings fund to the credit of the patient. The hospital also supplies clothing and other personal articles for the patient. Through physicians and social workers the hospital gives the patient adequate supervision and ensures his comfort and general welfare. The hospital receives from an appropriation 1.5 marks per day for each family-care patient; half of this amount is compensation for the patient and the balance is used to reimburse the hospital for the supplies and services furnished the patient.

The superintendent of the Mainkofen Hospital reports that its system of placing out patients is giving general satisfaction to both patients and families.

In Germany as a whole the male and female family-care cases are about equal. There is, however, considerable variation in the sex distribution in the several states. Likewise, the types of patients placed out differ in the various parts of the Empire. In general it is estimated that 60 per cent of the patients in family care are mental defectives, 35 per cent patients with mental disease and 5 per cent epileptics. It is claimed that in many cases behavior of patients is better in family care than in the hospital. So marked is the improvement in certain disorders that family care has come to be considered a valuable therapeutic measure. Placement in a congenial home gives many a discouraged patient new life and hope.

Close supervision of family-care cases is maintained by the hospital. As a rule, a newly-placed patient is visited twice a week by social workers and twice a month by a hospital physician. In emergencies a hospital physician immediately visits the patient. Whenever necessary, the patient is returned to the hospital.

Opinion in Germany is divided with respect to the advisability of boarding out patients in their own homes or the homes of relatives. Theoretically to pay a family for the care of a close relative is clearly objectionable. In Germany, however, the practice of placing certain patients with relatives is found to work satisfactorily. The family is compensated only when necessary and

10

the compensation in all cases is small. Whenever possible a patient who is able to return to his own home is paroled or discharged, but supervision over the patient is continued by the hospital for a considerable length of time.

In the following pages three outstanding developments in family care in Germany are described. Other variations in methods used are found in the several German states.

Experiments Made by Uchtspringe Mental Hospital

Following the opening of the Uchtspringe Mental Hospital in Saxony Province, Prussia, in the fall of 1894, it was found that there was a lack of suitable applicants for positions as male attendants. The superintendent, Dr. Konrad Alt, a leader in the promotion of family care, after a study of the situation, recommended to the provincial authorities the erection, in the open country about 1.5 kilometers from the hospital, of a group of cottages which would serve the double purpose of furnishing homes for married male attendants and of providing suitable accommodations for patients to be cared for in such homes. Through the erection of this little village, Dr. Alt expected to secure (1) a number of stable, reliable attendants, (2) good homes for a group of patients, and (3) development of interest in family care among the inhabitants of neighboring villages. The plan met with the approval of the provincial assembly and an appropriation for the erection of the cottages was made. In 1895, four double houses were built and a year later three more were added. Thus 14 dwellings were made available. The small village thus erected was called Wilhelmseich because of an oak tree planted by patients. Each dwelling comprised eight rooms of which six were designed for the use of the attendant's family and two for the use of patients. The latter consisted of a large room for two patients and a small room for one patient. Adjoining each cottage ample land for garden purposes was provided. Each attendant paid a small rental for his cottage and was compensated for the board and care of the patients in his home.

Care was taken in the selection of the attendants and patients who were to live in the cottages and the experiment was conducted under medical supervision. The results were excellent and Dr. Alt's expectations were fully realized.

Many requests for patients were received by the hospital from families in the neighboring villages that had observed the care of patients at Wilhelmseich. In extending the system an interesting modification of the usual methods of placement was made. In the town of Gardelegen, 14 kilometers from the hospital, 220 female patients were placed in family care and in the villages about Uchtspringe and Gardelegen within a distance of

25 kilometers from the hospital, 235 male patients were placed. In Gardelegen the hospital fitted up two buildings, a community house and a bathhouse. The community house, called a lazaretto, was used for the head nurse and assistant nurse. In addition to their rooms it contained a bathroom, a single room for patients, a dormitory for seven patients, a kitchen, storeroom, and a room for medical examinations and treatment. The bathhouse was arranged for men patients in much the same manner, with the addition of a large bathing section in which several bathtubs were placed. Here at stated times men patients and women patients in turn were weighed and bathed.

A six-seated automobile was used by the hospital in transporting patients from the hospital to their foster-family homes and from such homes to the community house and the bathhouse. The community house stood ready to receive any female patient that was required to leave her foster home for any reason. Temporary or emergency care was afforded and, if necessary, arrangements were made to take the patient back to the hospital. The nurses in the community house maintained a general oversight of the patients in their district. Adjustments of difficulties with guardians were made and patients returned to the hospital or transferred to other families when necessary. Two physicians in the hospital were especially charged with the oversight of the patients in family care.

The plan whereby a community house served as an intermediate station between the hospital and the foster homes worked to the satisfaction of all concerned, and the patients placed out by the hospital gradually increased until the outbreak of the World War. During the war and during the period of inflation which followed, the number of patients placed in these communities dropped from 455 to 122. Following the inflation period a gradual increase again took place.

DEVELOPMENT OF FAMILY CARE AT JERICHOW

In November, 1899, Dr. Konrad Alt, director of the mental hospital at Uchtspringe, submitted to the civil authorities a plan for the extension of family care in Saxony Province of Prussia. The plan included the building of a rural mental hospital at Jerichow with capacity for 150 patients. This hospital was to serve as a center from which patients would be placed in foster homes in Jerichow and the surrounding villages somewhat after the Gheel pattern. The plan was adopted and steps were soon taken for the erection of the hospital.

In order that no time be lost in placing out patients in accordance with the plan, a building in Jerichow was rented to serve as a temporary hospital center until the new hospital was ready for use. Within a week after the opening of the provisional hospital with 20 beds, 5 patients were placed in Jerichow homes and in the following year 45 patients were placed in 29 families in Jerichow and nearby villages.

Following the opening of the new hospital the placing of patients in family care was continued, and within five years the number so placed reached 200.

In common with other places, Jerichow suffered greatly during the war and the trying days that followed. However, the family-care system so favorably established here survived and in 1927 comprised 161 patients out of a total of 659.

Konrad Alt, after his successful experience at Uchtspringe and Jerichow, expressed his conviction that the extension of family care could best be furthered by the establishment of small central hospitals or community houses in favorable regions to serve as intermediate stations between the large mental hospital and family care. The development of family care in the greater part of Germany, however, has not followed this method.

Family Care Conducted by the Erlangen Mental Hospital

Perhaps the best-known system of family care in Germany is that conducted by Dr. Gustav Kolb, superintendent of the mental hospital at Erlangen near Nuremberg, Germany. The hospital at Erlangen serves a district with a population of 540,-000 and is equipped to care for about 1,000 pa-

tients. Only patients in need of active hospital
care are kept in the institution. All others are discharged, placed in their own homes or the homes
of relatives, under supervision, or boarded out in
the homes of families having no relation to the
patient. The boarded-out patients are kept on the
books of, and may be returned to, the hospital if
they have difficulties in living with the family to
which they are assigned. Patients placed in the
homes of relatives or in their own homes are discharged from the hospital under an arrangement
similar to parole in the United States. The institution maintains supervision over the patients until they are recovered or until they reach a self-
supporting status. Both the boarded-out patients
and the discharged patients are visited regularly
by physicians and nurses of the institution. Visits
are made more often to patients recently placed
or discharged than to patients who have become
adapted to their family homes. In 1932, the hospital had nearly 4,000 out-patients under supervision; of these, 130 were boarded in families unrelated to the patient.

When placing a patient in a family the hospital
makes a definite written contract with the family.
The service that the family is to render the patient
is clearly stated and the part the hospital is to take
in the care of the patient is definitely set forth.
The weekly compensation to the family is specified
in each agreement. The rate is not uniform but

depends upon the condition of the patient and the contribution he is able to make toward his maintenance.

The hospital has formulated a detailed set of requirements or regulations for the guidance of families receiving patients. These regulations which are given below in abridged form constitute an excellent summary of the methods used in Erlangen in placing patients.

REGULATIONS CONCERNING FAMILY CARE PROMULGATED BY THE ERLANGEN HOSPITAL FOR MENTAL PATIENTS

1. The superintendent of the institution enters into a contract with the head of a family, preferably with a house-owner who has no tenants, whereby one or two rooms are engaged for the use of patients. One or two, at most three, patients of the same sex are placed in one family. Other persons not members of the family may be received in the dwelling only with the consent of the superintendent of the institution.

2. Patients placed in the family remain wards of the institution and are under the responsible supervision of officials of the institution and the inspectors appointed by them. Any patient may be taken from family care back to the institution by order of the superintendent. In case of the removal of a patient another patient will be assigned to the family as soon as convenient. The superintendent will give attention to the requests and wishes of the foster family so far as possible. The head of the family is responsible to the superintendent of the institution for supervision and care of the patient.

3. Bed linen, patient's underwear, and other clothing for the patient will be furnished by the institution and will be replaced when necessary. On request of the head of the household, the institution will also provide furniture for the bedroom. The foster family is required to safeguard, so far as possible, the furniture and clothing supplied, to keep a list of furniture and clothing and to protect the interests of the institution and patients.

4. Washing and mending of bed and personal linen are to be done by the foster family. The repair of shoes is done by the institution.

5. The family is required to receive the patient as one of its members and to treat him and care for him in accordance with the regulations of the institution authorities. All possible precautions are to be taken to protect the patient from injuries and the family is to care for him when he is suffering from minor and transitory illnesses.

6. The foster family is required to deal kindly and justly with the patient. In no case is the patient to be punished. All compulsion of the patient is forbidden. The physician in charge will give instruction as to the liberty which is to be allowed each patient. Any violent treatment of the patient by the foster family will result in the cancellation of the contract by the superintendent.

7. The family shall employ the patient in accordance with the directions of the physician. The patient shall not be compelled to work by means of punishment or harsh treatment but the physician will withhold the usual pocket money from patients who are capable but unwilling to work. It is forbidden to employ patients at work that is dirty, strenuous or dangerous or that re-

quires much responsibility (such as driving a team on the highway). Each patient must be safeguarded during leisure time as well as during the time when he is engaged in active work. The loaning out of patients to work for others is allowed only by written permission of the physician. In general the foster family is not permitted to receive from patients or their relatives services or favors not provided for in the contract.

8. Patients are to live and eat with the foster family and during daily rest periods to have a place in the family sitting room. In winter the physician may order the patient's bedroom heated to a stated temperature.

9. The foster family is to provide proper lavatory facilities for the patient and to be responsible for the patient's cleanliness and for the orderly condition of the patient's clothes and the patient's room. Patients working outside the home are to be accompanied to their work. Whenever necessary, and at least every Saturday, the patient's underwear is to be changed. The patient's bed linen must be changed when necessary and at least once a month. On Sundays and holidays patients are to be dressed in their good clothes. Whenever necessary, and at least once in three weeks, each patient must be brought to the institution to be bathed, weighed and examined.

10. To what extent patients should attend church is to be decided by the physician. Visits to taverns and the use of alcohol are forbidden to patients. The physician will decide in regard to visits of patients to amusements which may be made in company with adult members of the family. At the approach of darkness patients must be in the house. In general, the house is to be

properly locked. The foster family is to avoid the use of alcohol in the presence of patients.

11. Noisy drinking parties of the family will constitute grounds for the cancellation of the contract. Persons, especially those of opposite sex, who come frequently in contact with the patient must remember that the patient enjoys special lawful protection and as a rule is not permitted to make contracts or to give away his belongings.

12. The foster family is required to report all untoward occurrences relating to the conduct of the patients, especially destruction of property, undue excitement, threatening expressions or behavior, stubbornness, wandering away, late home coming, use of alcohol, insomnia, refusal to eat, bodily sickness, etc. In urgent cases, report is to be made to the institution by telephone; in other cases, to the institution inspectors at the time of the first visit following the untoward occurrence.

13. The foster family is not permitted, without special permission, to have private correspondence with the relatives of patients or to impart information concerning patients or to receive gifts from relatives. Questions concerning patients are to be referred to the physician for answer. On Sundays, patients may be visited by near relatives and may write to them or receive letters from them unless such visits and correspondence are forbidden by the physicians. Visits to patients by others than close relatives are forbidden. Such visits are to be reported by the family. Relatives who show an inclination to take the patient home with them are to be reported.

14. Every working patient who renders services to the foster family receives monthly from the physician a graduated amount of pocket money, at least 10 pfennigs, at most, 50 pfennigs for each day. Payment is to be made on Sunday and receipt is to be obtained. The physician decides what amount is to be paid. The physician also determines what amount is to be paid out or used for purchases for the patient, and how much shall be deposited in the savings bank. Withdrawal of patients' funds from the savings bank is permitted only by written consent of the physician. From his pocket money, the patient is to receive regularly certain personal articles such as cigars, tobacco, writing material, stamps and tickets to amusements unless they are furnished by the institution. The accumulation by the patient of over five marks of pocket money is to be reported; likewise, the misuse of pocket money, that is, the purchase of beer, attendance at forbidden amusements, waste of money, etc., must be reported.

15. For rent of room and for board and other services, the family receives, for each patient, in accordance with his condition and requirements, graduated compensation of between a quarter and three-quarters of the per capita cost of the care of a patient in the institution. On the average the amount received by the family is about 1.7 marks per patient per day (1933). If the institution renders many services to the patient, the family receives correspondingly less. When a family cares for a patient without much assistance from the institution, the pay is greater. The monthly compensation to the family is paid from the treasury of the institution. However, a certain amount is held back to be used as a penalty in case the

contract is violated by the family. Such amount may be paid the family if lapse occurs in the period of care without the fault of the foster family. The institution in exceptional cases becomes responsible for property destroyed by patients if no blame attaches to the foster family. A family who has been successful in caring for chronic patients so that in the opinion of the physician they have been kept out of the institution many years is awarded a special premium or gift up to 100 marks.

16. A patient in family care does not obtain a settlement; he does not become taxable in the community in which he is placed and the family with whom he resides is not required to pay taxes on his account.

17. Patients placed in family care are not obliged to pay insurance premiums. In case of sickness or an accident, the institution bears the resulting costs and renders the necessary services. In case of death of the patient the responsible society or the responsible relatives bear the burial expenses.

18. All questions in dispute concerning the contract and regulations are decided in the first instance by the superintendent of the institution, in the second instance by the district authorities after a hearing before the district committee. Recourse to law courts is denied to both sides unless permitted by the district committee.

Evaluation of Family Care in Germany

That family care of mental patients has been advantageous to Germany during the trying years of the past two decades requires no argument. Patients, both within and outside the hospitals have benefited because of family care. Hospitals relieved of part of their burden have been able to do better work. Families receiving patients have improved their economic status and have had an outlet for their altruistic sentiments. Taxpayers through family care have been relieved of part of the burden of hospital maintenance and the building of new hospitals.

Further advantages were set forth by Dr. Ernst Bufe of Uchtspringe, at the International Congress on Mental Hygiene held in Washington in May, 1930. He presented the following 15 points:

1. Foster-family care is the most natural and the freest form of the placing of mental patients.

2. Foster-family care saves the patient from the mental damage done by prolonged institutionalization.

3. Foster-family care results in a quicker social readjustment of patients.

4. Foster-family care is for many patients a successful form of treatment.

5. Foster-family care guarantees individual psychotherapeutic treatment because it is obliged to individualize; institutional therapy is preponderantly mass therapy.

6. Foster-family care makes it much easier to give the patient change of environment and home conditions.

7. Many patients receive great psychotherapeutic benefits from being surrounded by persons of a different sex, by children, and by animal pets.

8. Foster-family care offers the patient numerous occupational possibilities, unequaled in naturalness and therapeutic value.

9. Foster-family care is the natural bridge to parole and discharge.

10. Foster-family care is an indispensable means for unhampered "early discharge" and for parole. All patients who for some reason cannot be placed in their own families should be put in foster families.

11. Foster-family care is the natural binding link between institution and parole, each facilitating the other's establishment and development.

12. Foster-family care is the cheapest treatment in the world. Every boarding patient makes the providing of a bed in the institution unnecessary. Also, the number of nurses needed is very low.

13. Foster-family care is an excellent means of popularizing psychiatric endeavors and of propagating mental hygiene knowledge.

14. Foster-family care of all three types can be introduced in all countries. It is also possible to have it in large cities.

15. Foster-family care is applicable for almost all types of patients.

CHAPTER IX

The Family Care System of Scotland

BY HORATIO M. POLLOCK

The establishments for the care of mentally-ill (lunatic) patients in Scotland on January 1, 1936, comprised 7 royal asylums,* 21 district asylums, 2 private asylums, 1 parochial asylum, 14 lunatic wards of poorhouses, and the criminal lunatic department of the prison at Perth. The total patient population of these establishments at the beginning of the year 1936 was 18,353. Compared to state hospitals in America the Scottish institutions would all be considered small. The largest asylum, the one located at Hartwood, had 1,486 patients; three others had respectively 1,249, 1,041 and 946 patients; the rest were all smaller.

Patients classed as ''lunatics'' cared for in private dwellings on January 1, 1936, numbered 1,257. The dwellings, although widely scattered throughout rural districts, villages and cities, are relatively most numerous in rural communities.

Mental defectives in Scotland are cared for in certified institutions or in private dwellings. In 1936, there were 14 institutions specially provided for this class of patients. Together, they housed 2,833. The number under guardianship in private

*In the annual reports of the General Board of Control of Scotland, institutions for the care of mental patients (with three exceptions) are called asylums and the patients are classed as lunatics. This accounts for the apparently antiquated terminology used in some parts of this chapter.

dwellings was 1,437.   Some mental defectives are
still cared for in asylums for the mentally ill but
no separate accounting of these is made in official
reports.

The annual report of the General Board of Control of Scotland for the calendar year of 1934 calls
attention to the serious overcrowding of the asylums, and makes the following statement:

"The only real hope of any relief to the congestion in
the asylums today appears to be along the line of an ac-
celeration of the boarding out of suitable patients under
private care and the extent to which that is possible will
partly determine the extent to which local authorities will
require to face the provision of additional asylum accommodation.   The system of boarding out in Scotland has
been attended with conspicuous success, and much credit
for that is due to the interest and enthusiasm of the Inspectors of Poor or Public Assistance Officers upon whom
have devolved the many and numerous duties of the selection of guardians and of associating the right patient
with the right guardian.   It is important that these officials should receive every encouragement in this part of
their work, and that they should be supported therein
by the public health officials and the asylum superintendents."

The system of family care referred to so approv-
ingly by the board dates back to 1857, but even previous to that time, mental patients were boarded
out by poor officials.

In 1855, Dorothea L. Dix, who had already accomplished wonders in the improvement of asy-

11

lums for the insane in the United States, visited Scotland as an ordinary tourist. While there she became interested in the Scottish asylums and on visiting them found very unsatisfactory conditions. Her findings naturally gave rise to much comment. Learning that a movement was under way to discredit her work in London, she proceeded to that city, saw Lord Shaftsbury and the Duke of Argyle and with their aid had a conference with the home secretary, Sir George Gray. The latter, after being informed concerning the situation, decided to appoint a royal commission to inquire into the "State of Lunatics and Lunatic Asylums in Scotland." A thorough inquiry followed. The report of this commission stated that there were in Scotland, 2,839 patients in public institutions, including 8 asylums, and 12 poorhouses with separate wards for the insane; 657 patients in 23 private establishments; and 1,363 in private houses. All types of care then in use were deemed unsatisfactory. The commissioners urged district boards to build new asylums and to license private homes, each home to care for not more than four patients. The following is an abstract from their report:

"That all cases of insanity should be placed in an asylum is a proposition we cannot entertain; the welfare of the patients would not thereby be promoted, while the expense to the country would undoubtedly be greatly increased . . . All great aggregations of permanently diseased units are evils which should, as much as possible, be avoided, as their tendency is undoubtedly to lower and degrade each constituent member of the mass. Viewed in a certain light, then, asylums may be regarded as necessary evils; . . . We would gladly see enacted, that any number of patients, not exceeding four, might be received into a private house . . . Under some such provision we feel satisfied that a system of cottage accommodation would gradually spring up, which would not only furnish more fitting accommodation for chronic patients than the lunatic wards of poorhouses, but would also be calculated to prove a valuable adjunct to asylums . . . The practical advantages of such a system would be, the greater amount of liberty accorded to the patients; their more domestic treatment; and their more thoroughly recognized individuality.''

In accordance with the recommendation of the commissioners, a supervised system of family care of mental patients was authorized by an Act Regulating the Care and Treatment of Lunatics which was passed August 25, 1857. From that time to 1913 there was an irregular increase in the number of ''boarded-out'' cases, the number reached in that year being 2,909. During the years of the World War there was a decline which has since continued at a slower rate. The reduction is partly accounted for by changes in classification. Some of the boarded-out cases formerly certified as ''lunatics'' are now certified as mental defectives. The number of the latter cared for in families increased from 555 in 1920 to 1,437 in 1936.

THE BOARDING-OUT SYSTEM

Although all certified pauper patients in Scotland are under the supervision of the General Board of Control, asylum treatment is practically separate from family care. Many of the patients in family care never see an asylum and the asylum superintendent does not know of their existence. A superintendent may recommend some of his patients for family care but after they are placed in family homes his authority over them ceases.

The administration of the boarding out system was formerly vested in parish councils, of which there were 875. In 1929, a new local government act was passed. This act, on the 15th of May, 1930, transferred to county councils and to town councils of large burghs the duties formerly exercised by district boards of control and by parish councils under the Lunacy and Mental Deficiency Acts. Accordingly, at present county councils or town councils select the guardians and homes that are to receive patients.

Standards of care and administration, and rules pertaining thereto are established by the General Board of Control, but the placing and oversight of patients devolves on the local officials. Moreover, the inspection by local officials is supplemented by visits by deputy commissioners representing the board.

A mentally-ill patient may be placed in family care in any one of the following ways:

1. Directly by local authorities with the sanction of the General Board of Control. The patient must first be examined by two physicians and both must certify to his mental illness.

2. By transfer from an asylum to a private dwelling on the certificate of the superintendent together with the sanction of the board.

3. A patient discharged from an asylum whose name is still on the parish roll may be placed in family care by local authorities with the sanction of the board.

4. A patient on parole from an asylum for any period up to a year, if he has not recovered at the expiration of the period, may with the sanction of the board, be placed in a family home.

The types of mentally-ill patients placed in family care are described by Dr. George Gibson, who was deputy commissioner for many years, in the following words:

"From a psychiatric standpoint they may not present many interesting features. The types of mental derangement most to be met with are mild and chronic manias, patients with harmless delusions, dements and patients showing the signs of congenital insanity from slight degrees of mental deficiency to idiocy. Suicidal and homicidal patients are naturally as entirely unsuitable for this method of disposal as are noisy, violent, restless and wandering cases. Epileptic patients must also be regarded with a suspicious eye, and though patients suffering from epilepsy may be permitted to remain at home with their relatives, they cannot be regarded as suitable patients to be boarded out with strangers. It is not fair to guardians to send them patients with unpleasant habits, or who from physical infirmities, are unable to look after themselves.''

As the success of family care depends fully as much on the guardians as on the patients, the former are chosen with great care. They must be substantial, intelligent householders of good character and habits. Their family life must be wholesome and all adult members must have a friendly attitude toward the patient when received in the home.

A guardian must have a dwelling large enough to furnish comfortable quarters for the number of patients assigned him. There must be adequate provision for heating, ventilation and light and the customary home comforts. In addition the guardian must provide suitable exercise, occupation and diversion for the patients in his care. A guardian can care for but one patient unless specially licensed by the board to receive more. The maximum number permitted to a dwelling is four; the numbers most commonly found are one and two.

Many of the Scottish guardians have cared for patients for years, some even have grown up with patients in the home. These guardians understand how to manage their "boarders" in order to make them useful and happy. The example of these successful guardians is a potent influence in maintaining the Scottish system on a high plane.

Although nearly a third of the mental patients in private dwellings in Scotland are boarded with relatives, the advisability of the practice may be questioned. It may be taken for granted that the qualifications required of relatives for the position of guardian are lower than those required of others and that standards of care in homes of relatives are not so high as in homes of strangers.

Inspection of Family-Care Patients

Although patients are cared for in separate homes without any attempt at grouping, an efficient system of inspection is maintained. Patients are visited every quarter by the district medical officer, and twice annually by the inspector of public assistance. In addition a deputy commissioner of the Board of Control visits each mentally-ill patient once a year, and each mentally-defective patient twice a year. Local inspectors record their visits in a book kept for the purpose in the home of each guardian. The inspectors interview the patients and their guardians, make thorough inquiry into the household arrangements, the food served the patients, the work required of them and other matters pertaining to the patients' comfort and welfare.

As the guardians know that they must maintain an adequate standard of care or lose their status as guardians, not many of them are found wanting. The inspectors naturally have many adjustments to make but the difficulties found in family care are probably not proportionally greater than those experienced in hospital management.

COST OF FAMILY CARE

The rate paid guardians for the care and maintenance of mental patients varies considerably in different parts of the country. In general, family care costs much less than institution care. The table given on page 169, which is taken from the annual report of the General Board of Control for 1929, gives comparative data of costs of the various types of care for eight consecutive years.

Data for later years are not given in the same way but the 1934 and 1935 reports give comparative figures relating to costs, as follows:

	Weekly per capita			
	1934		1935	
	Shillings	Pence	Shillings	Pence
In royal asylums	21	8	21	9
In district asylums	17	5	17	9
In lunatic wards of poorhouses	14	11	14	11
In private dwellings	13	3	15	1

THE AVERAGE WEEKLY COST OF MAINTENANCE OF PAUPER LUNATICS IN THE DIFFERENT CLASSES OF ESTABLISHMENTS, AND IN PRIVATE DWELLINGS, IN EACH OF THE EIGHT YEARS, 1921-22 TO 1928-29

	1921-22		1922-23		1923-24		1924-25		1925-26		1926-27		1927-28		1928-29	
	s	d	s	d	s	d	s	d	s	d	s	d	s	d	s	d
In royal and district asylums, private asylums, parochial asylums and schools for imbeciles	26	4	22	4	19	11	20	2	19	11	19	10	19	9	19	10
In lunatic wards of poorhouses	21	8	17	10	16	4	16	11	16	8	17	3	16	11	16	3
In private dwellings	12	6	13	4	12	10	12	5	12	1	12	6	12	3	12	1
General averages	24	2	21	5	19	3	19	5	19	3	19	3	19	2	19	3

In considering these figures it should be remembered that housing or investment costs are not included in the amounts given as asylum costs. The weekly investment charge varies in the several types of institutions but on the average is probably at least eight shillings. When this is added to the weekly asylum costs it is found that they average nearly double the cost of family care. The saving effected by boarding out of a patient is estimated at 36 pounds or about $180 a year.

EVALUATION OF SCOTTISH SYSTEM OF FAMILY CARE

In estimating the value of the Scottish system one must take into account the patients cared for, the guardians, and the general public. The testimony of deputy commissioners, medical inspectors and non-official visitors is strongly in favor of the system.

A few direct quotations culled from annual reports clearly show the attitude of the welfare officials. Dr. Kate Fraser, an officer of the Board of Control, wrote in 1933:

"I have much pleasure in testifying once more to the high standard of care bestowed upon the pauper lunatic and rate-aided mentally-defective patients under guardianship in private dwellings. I should like to draw special attention to the attitude of guardians towards the whole welfare of the patients under their care. Very few, indeed, consider their duty to be accomplished when they have complied with the regulations by providing suitable accommodation, suitable occupation, suitable food, and adequate supervision. They go much further and by stimulation, by arousing interest, by arranging for recreation and occupation for leisure time and by giving them a real home life they add materially to their happiness and frequently develop latent capacities, hitherto undiscovered. This applies more especially to the certified defective who responds readily to environmental influences and who, under such treatment, develops self-respect and comes to feel that, after all, he is of some use in the world and not a being apart as his previous treatment has so often led him to believe.

"The success in boarding out can be attributed to many factors, e. g., the selection of patients, the care and supervision exercised by the local authorities, the care and interest of the medical officers, and the careful selection of guardians. All these factors are important, but the real success is due to the guardians. Were it not for their infinite patience, understanding, kindness, and care, 'boarding out' would not have reached the high level at which it stands today.

"The benefits of boarding out, both of lunatic and defective patients, do not apply exclusively to the patients. I have noticed within recent years that the presence of such patients in the community is having a definitely educative effect. In areas where such patients are placed, people are ceasing to regard mental illness or mental defect as something to be shunned or feared. Greater sympathy and greater understanding is being shown by the general public, and a new and enlightened attitude is gradually being developed."

Dr. Aidan Thomson, deputy commissioner, writes in the 1933 report of the board:

"I have been profoundly impressed by the value and the possibilities of the boarding-out system. I consider it not only could but should be developed further. It fosters a root principle of human life, namely, the life in the family, which is accepted as a normal healthy unit. I do not think that any person would deny that he would willingly give up the electric light and other institutional conveniences with the abnormal life of the large group for a life with less material comfort in a small family unit. Surely a mode of life that runs along the normal course of national feeling must tend to greater mental betterment.

"It is on this principle that the boarding-out system is working, and it is a sound and proper principle.

"A basal factor in the public's attitude of doubt and questioning as to the benefit and value of boarding-out appears to be that the ordinary man does not realize that a person may be disordered in mind and even certifiable as insane, but that certifiability is not necessarily a reason for institutional care. This fact is emphasized when one sees some of the patients with their guardians. The patients are at times very disordered mentally; but one finds that the man or woman has been with the guardian 5, 10, 20 years and is very much a member of the household."

Dr. Ferguson Watson, deputy commissioner, reports in 1931:

"Generally, the care and supervision of boarded-out patients attains a remarkably high standard of proficiency. The great bulk of guardians have housed patients for many years. In numerous instances their children have been reared in the same house, have taken their food at the same table, have regarded the patients as part of the household, and had become so devoted to them that when a parent died a son or daughter took over the duties of guardian. Such instances are not rare, and there are in Scotland a great many guardians at the present moment who are grandchildren and even great grandchildren of the original guardian. Some of the most capable, the most devoted, and the most conscientious unrelated guardians are spinsters, whose chief object is neither profit-making nor a desire for the exploitation of cheap labor, but a genuine desire for companionship, and practical sympathy for those unable to guide their own lives.

"It is seldom that any adverse remark is made in respect to old, established guardians. They welcome the official visit, they keep their patients clean, they dress them well, supply a dietary which is generally much superior to that which the patient had at home, vary the meals in such a way as to prevent monotony, and while they exercise tact and discrimination in supervision and discipline, they allow that amount of freedom which cannot possibly be allowed to patients in an institution."

Whether the Scottish system of family care could be advantageously adopted in America is a question worthy of consideration. Massachusetts, when it first undertook the boarding out of mental patients in 1885, was guided to no small extent by the experience of Scotland. But family care in Massachusetts, although proving satisfactory for a limited number of patients, did not keep pace with hospital care and was not copied by other states. In the last few years since Massachusetts has made family care an adjunct of hospital care and vested the placement of patients entirely in hospital authorities, a marked increase in its family-care system has taken place.

In this country, it seems certain that the state hospital or institution under the general supervision of the state department must be the dominant factor in family care. The dominance of local authorities in Scotland is one of the weaknesses of its family-care system.

The Scottish system may also be criticized for failing to provide adequate psychiatric supervision of the mentally-ill patients placed in families. When patients are placed by a hospital physician, he knows their condition and can determine the medical attention they should receive. Provision for such attention can be made in various ways. The patient may attend clinics, he may call on the physician at the hospital or the hospital physician may visit him in his foster home. Nothing of the kind is provided in Scotland.

A further lack of the Scottish system is the supervision of family-care patients by social workers and occupational therapists. The dwellings in which patients are cared for in Scotland are so widely scattered that such supervision would be very expensive if not impossible.

Lastly, the Scottish system seems to forget the patients' need for social life. Some guardians, of course, provide a social outlet for their patients but nothing in the way of community activities is planned for by the system.

Although it is evident that the Scottish methods of placing patients in families is not entirely in accord with present standards, the system is worthy of careful study. It probably will be many years before hospital authorities in this country shall have developed guardians with the skill and devotion manifested by the wise, kindhearted and ever-faithful Scotsmen who are sharing their homes with their unfortunate fellowmen.

The fact of the continuance of family care in Scotland through more than eight decades is of itself strong evidence of its value as a supplement to institution treatment. The further fact that home care of mental defectives is notably increasing indicates that it is meeting public approval and proving advantageous to both guardians and patients.

REFERENCES

1. Annual reports of General Board of Control for Scotland, 1928, 1930, 1931, 1932, 1933, 1934, 1935.

2. Campbell, Robert Brown: The Development of the Care of the Insane in Scotland. Jour. Ment. Sci., Vol. 78, pp. 774-792.

3. Gibson, George: The Boarding-Out System in Scotland. Jour. Ment. Sci., Vol. 71, pp. 253-264.

4. Letchworth, William P.: The Insane in Foreign Countries. Chap. III, pp. 109-171. G. P. Putnam's Sons, New York, 1889.

5. Mitchell, Arthur: The Insane in Private Dwellings. Edmonston and Douglas, Edinburgh, 1864.

6. Riggs, C. Eugene: The Boarding-Out System in Scotland. Am. Jour. of Insanity, Vol. LI, pp. 319-329.

7. Stedman, Henry R.: The Family or Boarding-Out System— Its Uses and Limits as a Provision for the Insane. Am. Jour. of Insanity, Vol. XLVI, pp. 327-338.

CHAPTER X

Family Care in France

BY HORATIO M. POLLOCK

France has had more than 40 years' experience with family care of mental patients. Its colonies at Dun-sur-Auron and Ainay-le-Château, which are described in the following pages, have been successfully operated and have fulfilled their purpose in admirable manner.

For some unexplained reason this system of family care has not had the growth nor the wide adoption that would naturally be expected.

THE FRENCH FAMILY-CARE COLONIES AT DUN-SUR-AURON AND AINAY-LE-CHATEAU

The Council General of the Department of the Seine in France in 1890 recommended that a trial of family care of mental patients be made. Accordingly, a colony for women patients was established at Dun-sur-Auron in 1892 and one for men patients at Ainay-le-Château in 1900. The former had 1,193 patients in families on December 31, 1932; the latter was caring for 468 on the same date.

The organization of these colonies follows the Gheel pattern but both are much smaller than their prototype. Suitable patients are sent from the mental hospitals of the Seine to the colonies and when necessary a patient may be returned to the

12

hospital from whence he came. The patients placed in families in these colonies comprise mild cases of mental disorder of various forms including senile psychoses, psychoses with cerebral arteriosclerosis, dementia præcox, and chronic alcoholic psychoses; also some mental defectives of the imbecile or moron type. In addition to these more or less chronic types, some convalescent mental patients are given temporary care in the colonies. The latter patients are eligible for parole but have no relatives with whom they can be placed. In the selection of patients for colony care the colony physician cooperates with the hospital physicians.

Each colony has a center comprising a small hospital, bathhouse, storeroom and sewing room and other administrative services. At the head of the colony is a medical director. He is assisted by physicians, nurses, steward, chauffeur, housekeeper, etc. At Ainay-le-Château, the colony personnel numbered 16 in 1933. The ratio of employees to patients was about 1 to 29.

The Colonie d'Ainay-le-Château places patients in families in five communes, which are villages or country districts. In January, 1933, the distribution of family-care cases in the several communes was as follows:

Commune	Patients in family care	Population of commune
Ainay	201	1,357
Saint-Bonnet	47	1,129
Braize	26	341
Valigny	77	720
Isle de Bardais	67	646

Dr. J. Vié of the colony in an article published in the Archives Internationales de Neurologie for January, 1933, from which the above figures are taken, thinks that the colony could be advantageously enlarged and that in the average commune the number of patients that could be satisfactorily placed in families might equal one-tenth of the general population. As a practical way to enlarge the colony, Dr. Vié suggests the establishment of a day school for abnormal children in the colony center, which would be attended by children placed in families in the district. The other work of the colony would not be affected by the school.

From the colony center at Dun-sur-Auron patients are placed out in the city of Dun and in several annexes or suburban communities. In Dun proper about 600 patients are in family care.

As a rule, two patients are placed in a family but the average rate varies in the several communes. In Dun in 1933, the 600 patients were cared for by 260 families; in Valigny, 150 patients were in 85 families.

Supervision of patients placed in families in these colonies is conducted by assistant physicians and visiting nurses under the direction of the chief medical officer. In the colony at Ainay there are three visiting nurses and in Dun there are eight. All are men with the exception of two who are assigned to the annexes of Dun. Each visiting nurse has a specified district and is required to see each patient of his district at least once in 15 days. In practice, visits are much more frequent, most patients being seen nearly every week.

In visiting a home in which patients are cared for, the nurse inquires concerning the patients' health, their conduct and their occupations. He inspects the rooms occupied by patients, their clothing and meals.

The sleeping rooms of patients are required to be furnished as ordinary bed rooms. The furniture is supplied by the family. The patients' clothing is furnished by the colony but laundry work for the patient is done in the foster home. At the sewing room in the colony center clothing of patients is repaired. The visiting nurse, when making his inspection trips, must see that the clothing of patients is in good condition and that prevailing standards of living are maintained by the foster family. Men patients are shaved at least once a week and their hair is cut once a month.

Patients are expected to do some work for the family with whom they live but must not be forced to do so. Women patients assist in housework, do light work in the garden, and occasionally care for the younger children of the family.

The visiting nurse when making his rounds is equipped with first aid materials and a supply of simple remedies. He instructs the family in their use and in the hygienic care of the patient. In case a patient becomes ill he is seen by a colony physician or he may be brought to the colony infirmary. In exceptional cases of mental disorder when colony facilities do not suffice, a patient is returned to the hospital to which he was originally committed.

Physically-well patients in foster homes are also visited more or less regularly by the physicians of the colony. These check the activities of the visiting nurses, examine the patients, inspect the homes and make any adjustments necessary to secure the comfort and well-being of the patients.

Patients are given each month a small amount of money for personal expenses, the amount in each case being determined by the physician. They are also given writing paper, stamps, coffee and tobacco.

Caretakers or guardians of patients are paid at the end of each month. In 1933, they were receiving 7 francs per day for women patients and 7½ francs per day for men patients. At an appointed day and hour the caretakers come to the colony center or other designated place for their monthly pay. They bring with them patients' clothing that needs repairing or renewing. After being paid and receiving the required allotment of clothing, the caretakers submit requests or complaints concerning their patients. These are recorded by the visiting nurse and later given consideration.

The advantages and disadvantages of the system of family care above described are summarized by Dr. Jean Bode as follows:

"The disadvantages of family care may be separated into two categories:

- a. Disadvantages for patients: Suicides, escapes, exploitation of their work, drunkenness, insufficient food, uncontrolled correspondence, and infrequent visits from members of the family.
- b. Disadvantages for the community: Homicidal reactions, violence, indecent behavior, crimes, defamation, spread of contagious disease and enforced idleness due to work of patients.

"The most of these disadvantages do not exist. The return to the hospital of those that do not adjust to family care, careful selection of patients for placement and constant supervision prevent most of the antisocial behavior above mentioned. Violent reactions, escapes and suicides are very infrequent. Crimes and indecent behavior among patients almost never occur. The health of patients does not suffer under family care, their death rate is lowered and their longevity increased.

"The advantages are of three kinds:

- a. Advantages for patients: Liberty, return to normal life, reinstatement in a home, separation from hospital patients, awakening of affection, progressive adaptation to social life, mental reeducation, incentive to work and possibility of self-direction.

b. Advantages for the community : Amelioration of rural hygiene through medical advice, conferences of guardians, installation of bathing facilities, introduction of prophylactic measures, and improvement of economic status of rural inhabitants.

c. Advantages to welfare department : Reduction of expense and lessening of overcrowding in hospitals.''

It will be seen that the advantages far outweigh the disadvantages.

References

Vié, Dr. J.: Les Classes d'Anormaux dans les Colonies familiales d'Arrières. Archives Internationales de Neurologie, 52:1; Paris, 1933.

Vié, Dr. J., and Chanès, Dr.: Les Infirmiers Visiteurs des Colonies familiales d'Aliénés. Archives Internationales de Neurologie, 52:459; Paris, 1933.

Bode, Dr. Jean: Les Colonies familiales d'Aliénés. Reviewed in Archives Internationales de Neurologie, 52:276; Paris, 1933.

CHAPTER XI

Family Care in Switzerland and Hungary

BY HORATIO M. POLLOCK

Family care of mental patients in Switzerland was begun in 1901. The first placements of patients in families were made in the canton of Berne. The experiment proving successful, other cantons introduced family care in the following order: Vaud in 1904, Schaffhouse in 1907, Zurich in 1909, Soleure in 1925, Argovie and Bâle-Ville in 1929, St. Gall in 1931, and Valais in 1934. Although the other cantons do not have official systems of family care, many of their patients each year voluntarily welcome such care.

Placement of patients in families in all cantons that have organized systems is governed by special regulations. In most cases, the patient is first admitted to a mental hospital and is under observation and treatment for a time before his placement in a family is considered. If eventually deemed eligible for placement, a suitable home is found for him. While in such home he remains a patient of the hospital and can be returned to it whenever conditions render it advisable. In the canton of Zurich certain mental patients are placed directly in families by the official inspector for family care.

In several cantons, colonies which serve as intermediate stations between the institutions and family care have been established. These colonies are managed by nurses or attendants in the employ of the cantonal institution. The colonies vary in size, accommodating between 12 and 30 patients.

As in other European countries, family care in Switzerland increased during the years preceding the World War, declined during the war, and increased again following the war. In 1934, the number of patients in family care in Switzerland was sufficient to give considerable relief to the well-filled institutions for mental patients. Exact data are lacking for the cantons other than Zurich, but it is stated by Dr. H. Bersot* that a total of about 400 mental patients were placed in families in Switzerland in 1934.

The report of the inspector for family care in the canton of Zurich for 1934 shows that in that canton on January 1, 1934 there were 354 patients in family care. During the year 86 patients were placed in family care and 61 patients were removed, leaving a total of 379 patients in families on December 31, 1934. The average annual per capita cost of the maintenance of patients in families in 1934 was 478.86 francs. The cost per day was 1.39 francs. More than half of the cost was borne by the patients or their relatives.

*Que fait-on en Suisse pour les malades nerveux et mentaux. Page 150. Berne, 1936.

Many of the men patients are placed among farmers and are very helpful in carrying on the work of the farm. Some of these receive a small wage in addition to their maintenance. Others work for board only.

The patients placed in families comprise several different classes, including dementia præcox, chronic manic-depressive cases; paretics who have had malaria treatment, mental defectives and some epileptics. They are patients that are not dangerous to themselves or others, and that are easy to manage and supervise.

In the canton of Zurich a special organization known as the "Institution des Inspektorates für Familienpflege" was set up in 1909 to manage and supervise the placement of patients in families. The head of this organization is a physician on the staff of the well-known hospital Burghölzli at Zurich. The inspector decides what families are eligible to receive patients and what patients may be placed in families. He supervises the assignment of patients and their transfer and return when necessary. He also has charge of the financial arrangements connected with family care.

In some of the cantons a visiting nurse or an assistant social worker in the employ of the institution visits the patients in family care, adjusts their difficulties and gives assistance and advice to caretakers. Such inspection proves of great value in maintaining a high standard of care.

EVALUATION OF FAMILY CARE IN SWITZERLAND

The continuation and growth of family care in Switzerland constitute adequate proof of its value as an adjunct of hospital care. Additional testimony is afforded by the opinion of Dr. Hans W. Maier, medical director of Burghölzli. In a personal communication to the author he states that the results of family care are very satisfactory. It affords excellent care for many patients who have improved so that hospital treatment is no longer needed but who cannot live in full liberty in the community and do not have families of their own to care for them.

Dr. H. Bersot in the book above mentioned (Page 149) commends the Swiss system of family care and emphasizes the benefits derived by patients, the advantages gained by caretakers and the savings effected by the cantons.

The following regulations concerning family care in the canton of Zurich were originally prescribed in 1909.

REGULATIONS RELATING TO FAMILY CARE

1. Families who take a patient to board must agree to receive the patient as a member of the family in the home and at the table and must treat him at all times with friendliness and good will.

2. The family which receives a patient with a complete outfit of clothing must provide for replacement of worn-out articles of clothing and must mend other articles.

3. Adult patients must not be permitted to occupy sleeping rooms with children or with other persons of a different sex.

4. Patients who are willing and able to work should be given suitable employment. Restraint must be used only in emergencies and only with the approval of the Board of Inspection. Corporal punishment is forbidden.

5. When a patient leaves his foster home without permission the Board of Inspection is to be notified immediately. If the patient is likely to injure himself or others, notice of his escape must be sent to the nearest police station. In case patients become physically sick or unduly excited, a physician should be called. The expense of the medical service is borne by the Board of Inspection. The Board is also to be notified of all cases of bodily illness.

6. The payment for board is to be determined by agreement between the Board and the foster family. The care and supervision required by the patient and the ability of the patient to work are to be taken into consideration in fixing the amount to be paid.

Family Care in Hungary

Family care of mental patients was begun in Hungary in 1905. At that time the institutions for mental patients were greatly overcrowded and funds were not available for the construction of additional hospitals. The first family-care colony in Hungary was modeled in accordance with the Gheel plan and was established at Dicsöszentmarton. Later other family-care colonies were established. These were closely affiliated with institutions in accordance with the annex plan.

Care of patients in families proved popular and the colonies rapidly developed. At the time of the outbreak of the World War in 1914, there were about 1,800 patients in family care. These constituted about 17 per cent of the mental patients committed to public institutions. During the war the colonies rapidly declined. They further suffered by the demoralized condition of the country after the close of the war. Some of the colonies were entirely abandoned and others had but few patients. The total number of patients in family care in 1923 was reported as 114.

With the improved economic conditions which followed money stabilization, the family-care colonies again grew and additional colonies were formed in connection with state institutions. By January, 1930 the patients in family-care colonies had increased to 2,267, which comprised 26.4 per cent of all patients committed to mental hospitals.

Relatively, Hungary surpasses all other countries in the family care of mental patients. Apparently the system in use is well adapted to the country and is meeting popular approval.

At the First International Congress on Mental Hygiene held in Washington, D. C., May 5 to 10,

1930, Dr. Rudolf Fabinyi of Hungary discussed family care as conducted in his country and made the following comprehensive statement concerning the advantages of the system.

ADVANTAGES OF FAMILY CARE IN HUNGARY AS VIEWED BY DR. RUDOLF FABINYI*

"Family care has many important advantages:

1. It is advantageous to the state particularly for financial reasons. Patients are being cared for in a less expensive and at the same time better way; in Hungary the daily cost per person amounts to 28 cents as over against 55 to 88 cents in institutions. However, there is an even greater, though not immediately obvious advantage to be mentioned, for through family care much can be saved in the way of expensive extensions to existing institutions or the erection of new ones.

2. Family care has a strong and important influence upon the foster family and through them upon the whole neighborhood population. This influence is twofold: (a) material and financial and (b) moral and intellectual.

Very often the compensation money constitutes an important subsidy for the population of mostly very poor rural districts. There are war widows who live, aside from an extremely small piece of real estate, almost entirely upon the compensation money for two or three patients. It was possible for many families to make, by use of the compensation money, improvements in the house and the patient's room, for instance, to get proper wood flooring, better furniture, and the like. Several families have even received loans from their banker because of

*From Proceedings of the First International Congress on Mental Hygiene. P. 397. Used by permission of Secretary-General of the Congress.

the regular receipts of the compensation money; these loans they have used for building new homes.

Last year the amount of paid compensation money reached the sum of $210,525. Thus family care constitutes an economic advantage for the national prosperity, inasmuch as this great sum is directly commercialized and distributed generally and need not be used in the expensive administration of institutions.

Much more important, however, is the educational influence of family care. The effects of frequent contact with physicians and nurses, even the continuous living with the more intelligent patients are very noticeable in these families, especially in matters of hygiene. The people are being taught to lay floors in their rooms, to build larger windows and adequate toilets, and in general to live in more cleanly, healthy and hygienic ways.

3. The greatest significance of family care, however, lies in the effect that it has upon the patient himself, and in the fact that it constitutes the most adequate preparation for a reurn to free life, since it really trains the patient for this goal.

Although, for administrative reasons, family care is usually an outside department of an institution, there is a great difference between the two, since family care creates an entirely different environment. In family care the patients come again among "normal people" often back to their former living conditions, where they feel most at home. In institutional treatment, no matter how excellent it be and how active an occupational therapy department has been established, there is always more or less danger of generalization and mechanization. The most natural and the easiest road to individualization leads through family care. Further, in institutional treatment, as even in agricultural colonies, the patient is more or less, sometimes completely, isolated from the outside world; whereas family care places him under free life conditions with only a few restrictions. Thus family care is a powerful therapeutic method which, irrespective of its primitive nature, contributes to the difficult reintegration of our patients to social life to a high degree. As proof it may be stated that during the last year 60 patients recovered relatively, and 187 were released as improved, mostly persons who had obtained work and positions in the neighborhood and with the assistance of their colony.

In Hungary, too, we are placing under family care chronic cases who have already spent a long period in an institution, and who after an acute state of disturbance have reached a state of relative quietness. The number of these patients who are dangerous only relatively or only at times is very high, and they could not be handled through a parole system, especially when there are no reliable relatives.

We have also observed with great astonishment that these patients who in the institution are completely shut-in, autistic and inaccessible, often having bad habits and impulsive disturbances, mostly old schizophrenics and mental defectives, begin to become more active mentally, to work again, and gradually in time to return to normal life. Mental improvement is generally accompanied by physical gain. Although the food in the foster families is often simple and plain, the monthly weight charts show increase in weight, especially during the first months. The facial blood circulation and general healthy appearance are even more conspicuous. Fresh air and sunlight are needed by every one and these can be furnished through family care. For a number of years, family care of infirm and old cases has been tried. This led to improvement in their general condition. Unhappily little was accomplished with prolonged schizophrenics, although even the most untidy ones could be cared for in a family.

The good results with chronic cases led to experiments with acute cases. This resulted in remarkable improvement, even cures.

Eventually, patients who never had been in institutional care were entrusted to family care. Even before we knew of the experience with this type of care in Germany, an interesting number of such patients from the Budapest out-patients' departments who could no longer be managed by out-patient treatment were transferred to the family colonies at Balassagyarmat and Gyöngyös.

A close relation developed also with us between family care and out-patient department. Because the colonies mentioned are too far away for the Budapest out-patients' department, a new family colony was planned last year near Gödöllö at a distance of one hour by street car from the capital. Unhappily, financial conditions have delayed the construction of this colony.

All forms of mental illness are represented in family care. The highest percentage of cases, more than 27 per cent, belong to the schizophrenic type. The group of congenital mental defects constitutes nearly 20 per cent (a higher percentage than in the institutions), and general paralysis nearly 10 per cent (particularly many women), mostly cases that have gone through malaria treatment.

13

Then follow the epileptics, with nearly 9 per cent. For the manic-depressives, the figure is approximately 6 per cent; and for the paranoiac, including the paraphrenic, 7.5 per cent. As in the institutions, the number of senile dements has increased heavily in family care, making up 6 per cent. Relatively few cases of alcoholism occur, for men, 5 per cent; for women, 0.33 per cent. The number of cases of alcoholic psychoses is less in the institutions than in the pre-war period. It is relatively still smaller in family care because it is nearly impossible to make sure of a necessary abstinence in that type of care and treatment. In the colony Dicsöszentmarton, the method was introduced of hanging the photographs of the alcoholics on the walls of restaurants and saloons, with the official order that all serving of alcoholic beverages to these people was forbidden under the most severe penalties. This method has had the most desirable results.

In resumé, it can be stated that family care of mental patients has developed in Hungary to a high degree. This method of care of mental patients is not only a humane form of treatment, which gives the greatest possible amount of freedom, but it is an excellent system of therapeutics, which, moreover, can be applied without much expense. Family care must be regarded as an essential method in the treatment of the mentally ill, also as an important link in the chain of agencies that are used for the treatment of the mentally ill and the mentally abnormal. The types of care and treatment ought to follow each other in this way:

1. The mental health clinic.
2. The free neuropsychiatric division.
3. The mental hospital (closed wards).
4. The farm colony.
5. Family care.
6. Parole work (out-patient department).

Although family care has primarily a therapeutic task to fulfill and serves more particularly for reconstruction and the regaining of mental health, it is also important for preventive work. Already, for the reason that the people of certain localities are continuously occupied with the care of mental patients and are in contact with specialists, a very decided change in public opinion toward mental disease and its treatment has taken place. In such localities there is a totally different attitude toward mental patients and mental diseases. The psychiatrist is met with confidence; everybody likes to obtain his advice. This is very different from the situation in other places where there is still distrust.

APPENDIX A

Notes and Comments Concerning Family Care of Mental Patients in Various Places

FAMILY CARE IN NEW YORK STATE

The first institution to introduce family care of mental defectives in New York State was the Newark State School which placed a few patients in families in September, 1931. The development of this system of care by the institution is described by Dr. Charles L. Vaux in Chapter III of this volume. The experiment carried on by Dr. Vaux having met with success, the State Legislature in the 1935 session made provision in the appropriation bill for the allocation of a sum not to exceed $20,000 from the maintenance fund of each institution in the Department of Mental Hygiene for the purpose of establishing a system of family care for patients at rates not exceeding $4 per week. The funds thus allocated became available to the institutions July 1, 1935. During the year that followed beginnings in family care were made by several of the institutions of the Department. The progress made to September 1, 1936, is indicated by the accompanying tabulation:

The experience of Harlem Valley State Hospital is told in Chapter IV. Statements and comments by some of the superintendents or other officers of institutions introducing family care are given on the following pages.

PATIENTS IN FAMILY CARE IN NEW YORK STATE
September 1, 1936

Institution	Patients in family care
State hospitals:	
Binghamton	14
Buffalo	12
Harlem Valley	54
Hudson River	18
Manhattan	1
Marcy	23
Middletown	84
Rochester	8
St. Lawrence	33
Utica	27
Willard	9
Total	283
State schools:	
Letchworth Village	13
Newark	103
Syracuse	3
Wassaic	24
Total	143
Grand total	426

FAMILY CARE AT HUDSON RIVER STATE HOSPITAL
BY DR. RALPH P. FOLSOM, SUPERINTENDENT

During the past fiscal year, 23 patients have been placed in family care. Of this number, 5 were returned, so that on June 30, 1936, 18 patients continued to receive this kind of supervision. This number includes only those cases for which the hospital pays $4 per week. Patients who are working for their maintenance and a small wage are not included in this number.

The placement of patients has been conducted through our social service department under the immediate supervision of the parole officer. In the beginning, local social agencies were contacted and as a result the first applicants desiring to take patients into their homes came through the office of the Dutchess County Emergency Relief Bureau. All applications were carefully investigated and by June 30, 1936, we were using six homes in which 18 patients had been placed. With one exception, these homes were all located in Dutchess County, being within a distance of about 20 miles from the hospital. The most favorably located home was in a village only about nine miles from the hospital. Because of its favorable location, it is our intention, in the future, to increase the number of patients in family care in this community.

As the number receiving this form of care increased, responsibility and problems involved became proportionately greater. Considerable time and effort on the part of the social service workers has been required in visiting and supervising these patients. When ill they have been visited by one of our staff physicians, and this has occurred in several instances. Some form of recreation has been necessary and this continues to be one of our problems. Since three of the six homes being used for our patients are too far from the village for them to attend any entertainment, such as motion pictures, it has been advisable, when possible, to bring some of these patients to the hospital to attend the amusements offered there.

Efforts have been made to choose our patients carefully; notwithstanding this, however, 5 out of the 23 cases placed were returned to the hospital for various reasons. One woman returned because of a physical ailment, another because of more active psychotic symptoms and still another because she preferred to live at the hospital. One man left the home and was apprehended and returned and a second male patient was returned because of a behavior problem.

From our limited experience, it appears that our patients now receiving family care get more individual attention, have food which is adequate and which is perhaps more to their liking, and live more satisfactory lives. In some cases definite and noticeable improvement has occurred in their mental condition. In several instances paranoid individuals have become less so. A catatonic case has brightened up and has taken new interest in her surroundings and there has been evidence of improvement in other cases.

It is our feeling that it is not practical to have the homes too far apart or too far from the hospital. Several homes in a village only a few miles from the hospital appears to be the ideal situation and we believe that we have made a start to establish such a group in a nearby village. We hope that conditions will be such that we will be able to greatly increase the number of homes in this community. Perhaps, later on, if the number increases sufficiently, it may be feasible to have one of our employees live in this community and give at least part time to the supervision of patients placed in families.

So far we have met with no serious problems in caring for these patients in the different homes, and there have been no objections offered by people living in the neighborhood.

FAMILY CARE CONDUCTED BY UTICA STATE HOSPITAL
BY DR. RICHARD H. HUTCHINGS, SUPERINTENDENT

In December, 1935, the system of boarding out patients in private homes at family or State expense was inaugurated. This is a forward movement and although it throws a heavier burden on the physicians and social service staff, it offers much to commend it. While the trial period has not been long enough to draw conclusions, some good results can be reported. The following letter, received from a patient in a boarding home, expresses the feeling of most of those who have been given this opportunity.

> "I think it only right that I should thank you for making it possible to come to live with kindly people, where I could regain myself, and again do the things that I felt I could do well before my sickness. I enjoy the home life here and all that goes with a home, as homemaking was what I always liked and worked for, and, being deprived of that, suffered much. I think this was a happy way of solving the problem of my hopelessness and to help me by showing me a way to help others . . . "

REPORT OF PATIENTS BOARDED OUT DURING THE FISCAL YEAR
ENDING JUNE 30, 1936

Boarded out during period:	Male	Female	Total
Paid by private funds	7	4	11
Paid by State funds	13	11	24
Free homes	2	1	3
Total	22	16	38

Change of status in above groups:

	Private			State		
	Male	Female	Total	Male	Female	Total
Returned to institution	3	1	4	5	5	10
Again boarded out ...	1	..	1	2	2	4
Off boarding fund in jobs	..	..	..	2	3	5
Old age assistance ..	..	..	..	1	..	1
Died	1	..	1	..	..	..

In boarding homes June 30, 1936:	Male	Female	Total
Private	4	3	7
State	7	7	14
Free	1	1	2
Total	12	11	23

The homes are carefully selected in urban and rural sections, the personality of the family being the chief concern. The homes are visited once or twice each month by the social worker.

Our aim has been to resocialize young patients by boarding-home placement, to rehabilitate others who had no other mode of exit from the hospital, and in certain selected instances to place out individuals who would shortly become eligible for old age assistance. We believe that this system can be expanded with benefit to the patient and to the hospital.

Homes in Which Patients Have Been Placed by Buffalo State Hospital

BY DR. H. L. LEVIN, CLINICAL DIRECTOR

Since August, 1935, we have succeeded in working out family care for four men and eight women in five family care homes. The following is a brief description of the homes and the patients placed therein:

Home No. 1 is located in the outskirts of Niagara Falls. The owners are a middle-aged couple who seem unusually sympathetic and understanding. They had two or three large bedrooms that were vacant. The house is a very large one and the grounds about it are spacious. Toilet and heating facilities are ample. The owners felt they could not afford to accept but one or two patients as they feared that if they did so, they would be unable to obtain desirable occupants for their remaining rooms. They were willing to try the experiment of giving up their entire home to patients if we could find at least four suitable male patients. Realizing the difficulties inherent in having more than one patient in a home, and having in mind particularly the difficulties in supervision and the increased possibilities for friction among four patients, we hesitated before deciding to try the experiment. In August, 1935, four men were placed in this home. Of these, one, an alcoholic deterioration, adjusted very comfortably from the start, gave no evidence of any alcoholic interests, and is still there. One, an arteriosclerotic, was returned to the hospital in October, 1935, because of frequent arguments with his fellows. A second, also an arteriosclerotic, was returned on December 12, for the same reason. A third arteriosclerotic was returned on December 31, 1935, at his own request as he was opposed to radio playing in the home at any time. These three arteriosclerotics were replaced by one cerebral syphilis patient and two dementia præcox patients. No change of patients has been made in this home since December 31, last. The present group appears to be very comfortable and contented.

Home No. 2 is owned by two elderly but very capable and efficient women in the city of Niagara Falls; a large house set in a spacious garden lot in a desirable section of the city. The conditions there were quite parallel to those of home No. 1. In September, 1935, four women were placed there: one classed as alcoholic deterioration, two as dementia præcox, and one as arteriosclerotic. The arteriosclerotic was replaced by an elderly dementia præcox patient on December 26, 1935, because the former was unreasonably faultfinding. This was the only change made and everyone there now seems happy.

Home No. 3 is in a good residential section of Buffalo. The owners enjoy an excellent reputation. They have a spare room. They met with financial reverses and the steady certain weekly income is welcome. Since September, 1935, they have had a dementia præcox female, aged 24, who was quite indifferent for many months, but now is taking much more interest in herself and we are trying now to have her attend one of the adult education centers in her vicinity.

Home No. 4, in a very good residential section of Buffalo, is owned by a practical nurse. Since October, 1935, she has had a female patient with alcoholic deterioration, aged 69, and they are mutually satisfied.

Home No. 5 is in the outskirts of Niagara Falls. The owners are a young married couple with two children. The wife is the daughter of the owners of Home No. 1. Having observed the success of

the venture in her mother's home, her husband, a
handy mechanic and carpenter, working only part
time, and the wife being very capable and ambitions, she had the upper floor of her home remodeled to give ample space and bathroom facilities
for two people. Since November, 1935, two elderly dementia præcox females have obtained excellent custodial care in this home.

COMMENT ON FAMILY CARE

BY DR. JOHN R. ROSS, SUPERINTENDENT, HARLEM
VALLEY STATE HOSPITAL

My experience with family care of mental patients has been very satisfactory and it has made
me feel that the project has considerable possibilities for future development.

In order to establish a project in any hospital
district, those in charge of the hospital must first
be thoroughly convinced that the project is feasible. This is necessary in order to prevent a
waning of interest and effort as a result of encountering any unforseen and unpredictable obstacles during its establishment. When the foundations are laid the project gathers much momentum on its own credit and it is necessary,
therefore, to have suitable hospital facilities and
personnel to adequately train, select and place
the patients. As there is no formula, pattern or
given set of rules to follow, the personnel should
have not only a knowledge of psychiatry and psy-

chology but also a thorough understanding of practical economics and the ordinary problems of individuals and families in order to successfully place patients. One of the striking facts in connection with family care of mental patients is that patients in family care are happier and more contented in their new homes "be they ever so humble" than they were in hospitals with comfortable beds and modern equipment. They enjoy more privileges and freedom in more homelike surroundings. In addition many are able to earn a small amount of money with which to purchase minor necessities and luxuries.

The cost of maintaing patients in family care is less than in hospitals. The present allowance of $4 a week per patient provided by the Department for their maintenance in family care permitted the project to become established, but in all likelihood this amount will have to be somewhat increased if the project is to become extended to any great degree in the future. However, the costs will always remain less than maintaining them in hospitals.

In the light of my experience, the system of family care of patients is, in my opinion, a valuable adjunct and aid to mental hospitals in humanely providing for and re-establishing patients, many on a self-supporting basis. It is economical and will lessen the necessity of construction of new hospitals.

MENTAL PATIENTS PLACED IN FAMILY CARE BY ST. LAWRENCE STATE HOSPITAL, OGDENSBURG, N. Y.

BY P. G. TADDIKEN, SUPERINTENDENT

From the St. Lawrence State Hospital during the past year there were placed in family care 39 patients. Our first patient was placed on July 30, 1935. Seven of these 39 had to be returned to the hospital leaving at present 32 patients in family care placed in 14 different homes; 1 in each of 5 homes; 2 in each of 4; 3 in 1 and 4 in each of 4 homes. Five of the patients returned were unable to adjust; 2 developed acute surgical conditions; 1 had a volvulus and was returned for operation, and the other fractured one of his metacarpal bones when engaged in work about the farm. Both will be replaced as soon as their condition warrants it. In addition, 2 other patients were returned to the hospital because of acute medical conditions, but have been replaced in other homes following recovery from their illnesses; 1 had pneumonia and the other an attack of hypertension.

Most of our homes are situated in and about the village of Madrid, New York. This village has a population of 526 and its residents are chiefly retired farmers. The village is located about 22 miles from the hospital. The homes in

which our patients reside are mostly of the farm
type, comfortable, and do not contain all the modern conveniences. Our families are kindly and
take an interest in our patients far beyond the
material gain. In several instances the patients
have filled a need for companionship as shown
by the acts of kindness, consideration and
thoughtfulness rendered them by the families.
Patients have been taken out on visits, on shop-
ping trips, and have attended social events with
the families in whose homes they reside. The
people with whom they live have made gifts to
them of clothing, jewelry, tobacco, candy, etc.

Most of our patients assist with the work in
and about the household and it may be said that
they are truly members of the family. Among
the caretakers are four former employees of the
hospital; one is a former supervisor, whose husband is a retired baker, and two are former attendants. In addition, one is a graduate nurse
from another State hospital. We have placed
both sexes in the same home without any difficulty
arising. It is our belief, from observation of the
improvement in some of our patients, that family
care will prove a definite therapeutic measure in
the treatment of the mentally sick.

EXPERIENCE WITH HOME AND FAMILY CARE

BY DR. ROBERT WOODMAN, SUPERINTENDENT, MIDDLE-TOWN STATE HOMEOPATHIC HOSPITAL

Chapter 27 of the Laws of 1935 provided that "There may be allocated from the money appropriated for maintenance and operation of any institution in the Department of Mental Hygiene a sum not to exceed twenty thousand dollars, for the purpose of establishing a system of community care for legally admitted patients and inmates at rates not exceeding four dollars per week." Preliminary inquiry for suitable homes was instituted in advance and promptly on July 2, 1935, two patients were placed in a home in Middletown, N. Y. Other homes were soon utilized and by the end of the first month 14 women patients had been placed. The earlier placements were made in and about Middletown but as the number of satisfactory homes willing to receive patients at four dollars a week was limited under the semi-urban conditions of Orange County, applicants from Delaware County were investigated and in the spring patients were placed in and about Shavertown. On June 30, there were 27 men and 39 women, a total of 86, under supervision in 27 boarding homes. Eighty were maintained from State funds and 6 from private funds but under the same supervision. The average number in family care during

14

the year was 38. Fifteen of the boarding homes in use at the end of the year and 41 of the patients were in Orange County, 11 homes and 44 patients were in Delaware County and 1 home with 1 patient in Ulster County.

Patients selected for family care have been predominantly of mature years and long in the hospital. The period of hospital residence may be seen in the following table:

Time in hospital	Number
Less than 1 year	5
From 1 to 5 years	13
From 5 to 10 years	19
From 10 to 20 years	24
From 20 to 30 years	17
From 30 to 40 years	5
From 40 to 50 years	3
	—
	86

Only a little more than one-fifth of the patients were under 50 years of age as appears by the following table of ages:

Age in year	Number
20 to 29	5
30 to 39	5
40 to 49	8
50 to 59	27
60 to 69	23
70 to 79	16
80 to 89	2
	—
	86

Patients on the Cornell Farm at Shavertown, N. Y.

A Group of Patients After a Long Winter at the Travis Farm, Howells, N. Y.

Five boarding homes were discontinued during the year. One with six patients was terminated by the death of the woman in charge; one by physical disability of the home keeper; one by an unsatisfactory family situation which led to giving up the home and moving to unsuitable quarters; one by moving too far away, and one from lack of understanding of the patients. Besides, one woman private patient was boarded alone in four different homes during the year and moved three times, either because of her own dissatisfaction or the dissatisfaction of the people with whom she was staying, or both.

Twenty-eight patients, including those whose homes were discontinued, were brought back to the hospital. One had to return temporarily for an operation, two graduated to parole with relatives, three had relapse of mental symptoms, five were after trial found dissatisfied or unsuitable. One woman and three men left their boarding places and four were ill or feeble. Twelve of the 28 returned for one reason or another subsequently went back to the same or other homes and were out at the end of the year. Only two had two unsuccessful trials.

Nothing serious occurred with any of the cases returned. One did not like the country and broke two or three dishes so she would be sent back. Two others talked at night. One man, now successful in another home, "could not live with a nagging woman." Those who left their boarding homes came to no harm. One woman classed as assaultive in two boarding homes was no problem at the hospital before boarding out and has been none since. Such freedom from difficulties is doubtless due in a large measure to careful selection of cases and the fear of complications may well have been exaggerated at the start.

One question that must inevitably arise is "Can patients get adequate food when only four dollars a week is paid?" Only four patients were returned because of illness and two of them are out again. Two who were permanently returned were feeble old women who succeeded for several months in one home nearby but were not strong enough to remain safely in another home 75 miles from the hospital. Patients have regularly expressed themselves as satisfied with their food and often are much pleased with the change from hospital fare. Those who have been many years in institutions especially appreciate home cooking and a family table. Meals have been inspected often by representatives of the hospital and the condition of the boarders has been watched. Many of them have gained weight. So little sickness among so many elderly people indicates good care and adequate nutrition.

Another fear has been that patients would be taken in as unpaid laborers. Most of those in families are able to help with their own care and they are encouraged to do so and the men in several instances to help some with the family labor. It is hoped that some may establish connections that will make them self-supporting but to date none have succeeded in holding work at wages although a few men have tried positions. No instance of exploitation or overwork has been found.

A program of community care cannot be a success unless the patients like it, and they do like it. Very few patients have wanted to return to the hospital. Many have expressed themselves strongly in favor of remaining outside. Some are indifferent or see the advantages and disadvantages in either procedure. Children, animals, pets, gardens, all add to the interests of home life and react favorably upon the patients themselves. It is surprising too in how short a time the home keepers become attached to their patients and humor their foibles, rejoice in their successes, guard against their weaknesses and champion their cause.

It is on these grounds of human values for selected patients that family care should primarily be judged. There is a money saving too although it is difficult to estimate exactly how much, for in addition to the four dollars a week paid in cash for maintenance, clothing has been furnished by the hospital and distributed by social service activity. Twenty-five cents a week for spending money for soap, toothpowder, postage stamps, moving pictures or whatever the recipients choose to use it for has also been allowed in most cases. Often this has been accumulated to buy stockings, a straw hat or other articles of clothing. The cost of supervision is considerable. Dr. Percival H. Faivre has given a large share of his time to this activity during the past year and much of the success so far obtained is due to him and to Maysie T. Osborne, chief social worker, who has made investigations of prospective homes and handled many details of getting the movement under way. She carried the social service work alone until October, when its expansion required the appointment of an assistant. Considerable transportation cost is involved, especially when the homes are 75 to 80 miles from the hospital, as they are in Delaware County. The patients in families are the ones who were least trouble and least expense to the State while they were in the hospital and in many instances were useful workers in the care of other patients. While they are easy to care for they can remain in the families where they now are but we anticipate that whenever they require much care, be it from old age, illness or reactivation of mental disease, they will be back in the hospital. On all of these grounds it is not quite pertinent to compare their cost in their boarding homes with that of the average patient resident in the institution. However, it can safely be said that each patient in a family saves the capital cost of building one additional institutional bed with its overhead, repairs and depreciation. After one year of experience we are in position to see many positive virtues in family care and to realize that on the contrary it is unsuitable for the larger fraction of State hospital patients, no cure-all for overcrowding and applicable only to special patients under special situations. Doubtless it could be extended here under present economic conditions to more patients than $20,000 per year will maintain at four dollars a week.

FAMILY CARE IN PENNSYLVANIA

The legislature of the state of Pennsylvania in the session of 1935 passed an amendment to its Mental Health Law providing for the boarding out of mental patients. The amendment reads as follows:

Section 627.--The superintendent and the board of trustees of any state mental hospital may, by contract or otherwise, arrange for the boarding out of such committed mental pateints who have not criminal, suicidal, or homicidal tendencies, who are not addicted to the use of alcohol or narcotics, and who in the opinion of such superintendent and board of trustees may be otherwise suitable. Such arrangements shall be made only with the approval of and subject to regulations prescribed by the Department of Welfare.

Such patients shall be deemed as remaining inmates of the state mental, hospital and shall be considered on parole subject to return to the hospital should the condition of the patient or other circumstances in the opinion of the superintendent and the board of trustees make such return necessary.

Subject to the approval of the Department of Welfare, such patients may, if physically and mentally able, earn the cost of their maintenance or a portion thereof by engaging in suitable employment. Provided, however, that such patients, who are physically or mentally or for economic reasons unable to earn the full cost of their maintenance, shall be maintained in the manner now provided by law with regard to indigent patients committed to state mental hospitals.

Under the guidance of the Bureau of Mental Health of the State Department of Public Welfare a start has been made in the placing out of patients as provided for by this amendment.

Previous to the enactment of the amendment, Dr. J. Allen Jackson, superintendent of the Danville State Hospital at Danville, Pennsylvania, had instituted a system of boarding out mental patients in cooperation with poor authorities. A description of the methods used by Dr. Jackson is given in the following statement written by him to the editor of this volume, under date of October 21, 1935:

"About three years ago we began the development of a plan for the care in the community of certain groups of mental patients for whom hospital care and treatment were no longer deemed necessary and for whom suitable placement could not be made with the immediate relatives.

"For this purpose three types of homes were sought:

1.   Wage homes in which the maintenance of the patient would be provided for entirely by his own labor.

2.   Part wage homes in which the work of the patient could be accepted as part payment for maintenance.

3.   Boarding homes in which maintenance would be provided by relatives, friends, overseers of the poor or county commissioners.

"In the selection of boarding or wage homes, great care is exercised to determine the community environment, the physical qualities of the home and the qualifications of the applicants for rendering the type of supervision necessary for patients placed with them * * * A social service investigator personally investigates the home and checks carefully on all references given, after which the home is either approved or disapproved by the superintendent of the hospital.

"The funds necessary to maintain an indigent patient in a strictly boarding home are $18 a month, which sum is divided into $14 for food and shelter and $4 for clothing and incidentals. This amount is provided by either relatives, friends, or, and in most instances, by the Overseers of Poor and County Commissioners of the district responsible for the maintenance of the patient in the hospital.

"In selecting the cases for family placement, careful consideration is given by the medical staff to each individual case and the principal groups so placed in the past have been chronic cases in which psychotic symptoms are not reflected in the conduct of the patient, senile and arteriosclerotic patients who are ambulatory and require only home care, while for the full-wage and part-wage homes patients of the trusted hospital working groups have been selected. Care is also exercised in the fitting of individual patients into the types of homes best adapted for that special type of individual.

"In a number of instances, patients have been placed with the families of nurses or former nurses of the hospital in some instances overseers of the poor have taken patients into their own homes, while the majority of patients so placed have been located in rural communities.

"After placement these patients report once monthly to the psychiatrist in charge of the mental health clinic nearest to their boarding home and the social investigator makes frequent personal contacts with the home.

"These patients on the whole have been well received in the communities where they have been placed and as a matter of fact the adjustments made by them have really been better than the adjustment of the group of patients as a whole that have been furloughed to their relatives.

"During the three years in which this plan has been in operation, 72 patients have been placed and but 12 have been returned to the hospital because of inability to adequately adjust."

THERAPEUTIC VALUE OF FAMILY CARE

COMMENTS OF DR. WILLIAM A. BRYAN

Dr. William A. Bryan, superintendent of Worcester (Mass.) State Hospital, who has had several years experience in placing patients in families, makes the following statement concerning the therapeutic value of family care.

"While the boarding-out plan of caring for mental patients does result in a saving represented by diminished capital expenditure for new buildings, yet I believe the major potentialities lie in the therapeutic field. There are many patients in state hospitals who are inmates apparently because of precipitating factors in their immediate environment, the home. We have usually found it necessary to return many patients who are convalescing satisfactorily directly back into an unhealthy situation. It has seemed to us much better practice to utilize our boarding homes as a first step toward complete emancipation from the hospital influence rather than to return patients directly to what cannot help from being a most trying situation for the patient. We hope that this plan will eventually result in a lowering of the readmission rate.

"Practically every large mental institution has numerous "hospitalized" patients, many of whom represent the most productive patient workers. A tendency exists to permit these patients to stay on in the hospital indefinitely. The boarding-out system offers an opportunity to eliminate this pernicious practice by forcing the patient from the institutional atmosphere back to a more normal family life.

"Again, there is a relatively large group of elderly patients for whom active institutional treatment is not indicated. While many of these patients cannot be satisfactorily cared for at their own homes they prove entirely amenable to a less expensive form of treatment in a boarding home and we are sure that in properly selected homes the patients are more happy.

"In brief, I thoroughly believe in the possibilities of this form of treatment for certain types of mental patients, providing adequate social service and medical supervision can be extended to the patients. Even if the per capita cost of this type of care should slightly exceed the institutional per capita cost it should be given a trial. It is entirely possible that satisfactory boarding homes may become more difficult to find as the economic situation of the country improves. It is conceivable, however, that under such a plan the incidence of readmission will be lowered and that in the long run the boarding-out plan might prove economical even although operating at a higher per capita cost than obtains in the institution.

"Another matter of paramount importance is the building up of a community responsibility for these patients. With the assumption of a partial responsibility for the care of patients by a community there should result a better and more understanding attitude toward the mental disease problem. The stigma so frequently attached to these patients and their relatives might gradually be diminished and possibly even eliminated.

Law Relating to Family Care of Patients in Utah Which Became Effective March 14, 1935

Section 2.   Patients Placed at Board.

The board of trustees of the hospital upon the recommendation of the superintendent may place at board in a suitable family in this state any indigent patient in the hospital who has been regularly committed and is quiet and not dangerous. Any such patient so placed at board by the trustees thereof shall be deemed to be an inmate of the hospital. The cost to the hospital for placing such patient at board shall not exceed $4 per week for each patient. The bill for the support of the persons who are placed at board in the families by the board of trustees shall be paid monthly by the hospital and shall be made out by the steward, examined by the board of trustees at their regular meeting and if approved, submitted to the state auditor as are other obligations of the hospital.

The placing at board of such patients shall in no way affect the rights of the hospital to supervision and readmission of the patients. All patients so placed at board shall be at the expense of the hospital and shall be visited by the superintendent or his duly appointed assistant at least every three months. Frequent reports may be required from those into whose care patients are placed by the superintendent.

APPENDIX B

Forms for Institution Use in Administering Family Care

The following forms are suggested for the use of state institutions which place patients in family care:

FORM 1. ADMINISTRATIVE INDEX CARD. This card may be used for administrative purposes and will be found useful for the maintenance of a systematic record of patients placed out. Two files of this card should be kept, one an active file and the other a file of cases removed from family care. The former would afford immediate reference concerning any case in family care. The latter would provide data concerning cases who had been in family care but had been removed or discharged, or had died.

FORM 1

FAMILY CARE

NAME OF PATIENT

Idem. No.   Male   Female

Residence   Diag.

Age   Relig.   Single
                             Married   Race   Last admit.   19
                             Widowed
                             Separated

Corresp.:

On   19   , placed with

Address

Wkly rate   , Paid: By institution—By relatives—By committee

Returned to institution   19

Paroled—discharged—died: 19

Comment:

Duration of prior placements (Use back of card)

15

FORM 2. APPLICATION FOR FAMILY-CARE PATIENTS. This form would be filled out by a family desiring to receive patients in its home.

FORM 2

APPLICATION FOR FAMILY-CARE PATIENTS

....

.... 193....

To the Superintendent of

.................................,...............

Dear Sir: I desire to care for   patients of your institution in my home for compensation and am submitting herewith information for your guidance in considering my application.

1. Location of home

    No.   Street   city or village

    If in country—Postoffice   Road

    Distance and direction from nearest village or city

    Telephone number, if any

2. Type of house (Underscore words that apply) Brick, wood, detached, joined with others, apartment, one-story, two-story, three-story

    Number of rooms in house

    Number of sleeping rooms available for patients

    On what floors

3. Conveniences in house. Specify which of the following conveniences are in your home:

    Bathroom

    Water closet

    Lavatories with running water

    Electric lights

    Furnace

4. Composition of family in home

Names	Ages	Occupation

5. Are all members of your family who are living in the home in good health? If not, specify illnesses

6. Are there persons not members of the family living in the home? If so, are they relatives, boarders or hired help?

7. Church affiliations of applicant

8. Names and addresses of three persons to whom reference may be made

9. Reason for desiring to care for patients

                                    Signature of applicant.

FORM 3. SOCIAL WORKER'S REPORT CONCERNING APPLICANT FOR FAMILY-CARE PATIENTS. This form gives an outline for the social worker's report concerning her investigation of the home of an applicant.

FORM 3

.... State ....

SOCIAL WORKER'S REPORT CONCERNING APPLICANT FOR FAMILY-CARE PATIENTS

Date of report

.... 19....

Name of applicant   Date of application

Address   Telephone number

Directions for reaching home

Composition of family

Character and economic status of family

Attitudes of members of family toward each other and
    toward caring for patients

Comment of references

Religion of family   Race

Type and sex of patients desired

Description of home and surroundings including number
    of rooms, modern conveniences, etc., and facilities for
    care of patients

Character of neighborhood

Rate of pay desired

Recommendation of social worker with reasons therefor

Signature of Social Worker

FORM 4. GENERAL INSTRUCTIONS TO CARETAKERS. This form includes the principal directions which should be given to every family receiving patients in its home.

FORM 4

GENERAL INSTRUCTIONS TO CARETAKERS

The following instructions have been prepared for the guidance of families who receive patients in their home. In matters not covered by the instructions it is expected that caretakers will use their best judgment and will consult the officers of the institution whenever necessary.

1. Home care. The patients placed in your home are wards of the State and are entrusted to you with the expectation that you will give them good care and make them feel at home in your family.

2. Meals. Patients should be given three meals each day. The food should be wholesome and of sufficient variety and quantity to maintain health and vigor. Marked changes in weight of patients should be reported to the social worker of the institution. If a patient refuses to eat for more than a single day, the matter should be reported to the institution.

3. Bed. Each patient must be provided with a separate, comfortable bed in a well-ventilated room. In rooms of sufficient size, two or three beds may be placed.

4. Clothing. Patients' clothing is furnished by the institution or by relatives. Caretakers are required to see that it is kept clean and in good repair. Patients when able may assist in care of clothing.

5. Work. Patients when physically able should be encouraged to do some work each day. Women patients may assist in housework and light outdoor occupations. Men patients may do chores, care for farm animals and assist in other farm and garden work. In addition, work projects may be furnished patients by the occupational therapist of the institution. No patient should be permitted to work beyond his strength or endurance, or to work for other families except by permission of the institution.

6. Play and other diversion. Some form of diversion should be provided for patients. Books and papers should be made available to patients who desire to read. The institution may assist caretakers in supplying appropriate reading matter for patients. Outdoor activities in suitable weather should be encouraged. Games such as cards, checkers and dominos, should be furnished for patients who desire to play them. Occasional social parties or other entertainments are highly desirable. Church attendance should be encouraged when practicable.

7. Bath. Bathing facilities must be provided for patients. Every patient must have free access to a lavatory and have a thorough bath at least once a week.

8. Supervision. Patients must be carefully supervised and a responsible person must be in charge of them at all times.

9. Discipline. Patients must never be punished or locked in their rooms. Kind treatment and gentle persuasion will accomplish much more than harsh measures.

10. Illness. If a patient becomes sick or is injured the institution should be notified at once. In an emergency a local physician should be called.

11. Absence. If a patient wanders away from your home a search for him should be made. If he cannot be found the institution should be notified.

12. Troublesome patients. If a patient becomes too troublesome for you to manage, the institution should be notified at once.

13. Visits. Patients must not leave your home to visit relatives or friends without written permission from an officer of the institution. A record should be kept of all visits to patients in your home.

14. Official visits. Official visitors from the institution when calling on patients in your home may desire to talk privately with each patient and to inspect patients' clothing and rooms. Such inspection is required by the institution and is in no sense a reflection on you or on your care of the patient.

15. Peculiarities of patients. Caretakers should discourage undesirable habits or tendencies of patients but should not laugh at their peculiarities nor discuss them with others.

16. Cooperation. Caretakers and the members of their family are expected to cooperate with the institution in promoting the well-being, happiness and recovery of patients. It is believed that much may be accomplished toward these ends by making the home life of the patient as comfortable and congenial as possible.

Superintendent.

BIBLIOGRAPHY

Alt, Konrad: über familiäre Irrenpflege. 80 pp. Halle a. S., 1899.

——: Die familiäre Verpflegung der Kranksinnigen in Deutschland. Halle a. S., 1903.

——: Weiterentwicklung der familiären Verpflegung der Kranksinnigen in Deutschland seit 1902. Halle a. S., 1907.

Bersot, H.: Que fait-on en Suisse pour les malades nerveux et mentaux, pp. 170, Berne, 1936.

Blumer, G A.: The Care of the Insane in Farm Dwellings. Am. Jour. Insanity, 56;31-40, July, 1899.

Bode, Jean: Les colonies familiales d'aliénés. Thèse, Paris, 1933.

Bothe, A.: über Familienpflege Geisteskranker nach den in Dalldorf mit dieser Einrichtung gemachten Beobachtungen. Allg. Ztschr. f. Psychiat. 49:650-668, 1892-93.

Brown, S. C.: Visit to Gheel Colony, Belgium. Ment. Welfare, 14: 1-7, Jan. 15, 1933.

Bufe, E.: Die Familienpflege Kranksinniger im heutigen Deutschland, ihr Stand vom 1, Oktober, 1927, ihre Schicksale in der Kriegs und Nachkriegszeit sowie ihre Beziehungen zur offenen Fürsorge. Psychiat.-Neurol. Wochnschr. 30:159, April 21, 1928; 173, April 28, 1928.

Burdette, V. M.: Experiment in Boarding Out. Ment. Welfare, 15:33-39, April, 1934.

Campbell, R. B.: The Development of the Care of the Insane in Scotland. Jour. Ment. Sci., 78:774-792, 1932.

Chanès and Vié, J.: Les colonies familiales d'aliénés du Département de la Seine. Rev. d'hyg. 55:281-296, April, 1933.

Copp, Owen: Further Experience in Family Care of the Insane in Massachusetts. American Jour. of Insanity. 63:361-375, Jan., 1907.

Crockett, H. M.: Boarding Homes as Tool in Social Case Work with Mental Patients. Ment. Hyg. 18:189-204, April, 1934.

Deperon: Du patronage familial des aliénés à Lierneux en 1897. Bull. Soc. de méd. ment. de Belg., Gand et Leipz., pp. 159-172, 1897.

Evans, A. E.: Tour of Some Mental Hospitals of Western Germany. J. Ment. Sci. 79:150-166, January, 1933.

Franks, R. MacL.: The Extramural Care of the Mentally Ill. Canad. Pub. Health Jour. 24:330-336, 1933.

Gibson, George: The Boarding-Out System in Scotland. Jour. Ment. Sci. 71:253-264, April, 1925.

Griesinger, W.: Über Irrenanstalten und deren Weiterentwicklung in Deutschland. Arch. f. Psych. 1:8-43, 1868.

——: Über die familiäre Irrenverpflegung. Allg. Zeitschr. f. Psych. 22:390-93.

Jankowska, H.: Familial Care of Mentally Diseased. Polska Gaz. Lek. 13:651-652, September 2, 1934.

Janssens, G.: Family Care of Insane. Psychiat. en Neurol. Bl. 39:418-436, May-June, 1935.

Jolly, F.: Ueber familiäre Irrenpflege in Schottland. Arch. f. Psych. 5:164-188, 1874.

Kilgour, A. J.: Colony Gheel. Amer. Jour. Psychiat. 92:959-965, Jan., 1936.

Knab, K.: Die Bedeutung der Familienpflege in deutschen Geisteskrankenversorgungs System. Psychiat.-Neurol. Wochnschr. 37:265-269, June 8, 1935.

——: Entwicklungsstand der Tapiauer Familienpflege. Allg. Ztschr. f. Psychiat. 96:339-347, 1932.

——: Familienpflege und Gesetz zur Verhütung erbkranken Nachwuchses. Psychiat.-Neurol. Wochnschr. 36:13-14, Jan. 13, 1934. *Abstr.* Centralbl. f. d. ges. Neurol. 71:428, 1934.

——: Plädoyer zugunsten der Familienpflege. Psychiat-Neurol. Wochnschr. 34:217-221, Apr. 30, 1932. *Abstr.* Centralbl. f. d. ges. Neurol. 64:837, 1932.

———: Statistik über den Stand der Familienpflege der öffentlichen deutschen Heil-und Pflegeanstalten im Sommer 1932. Psychiat.-Neurol. Wochnschr. 35:196-203, Apr. 22, 1933.

Kolb, G.: Psychiatrischer Entwurf zu Richtlinien für die Aussenfürsorge in Bayern. Allg. Ztschr. f. Psychiat. 88:433-448, April 21, 1928.

———: The After-Care in the Mental Hospital of Erlangen, Bavaria, Germany. Jour. Nerv. and Ment. Dis. 62:141-143, August, 1925.

Korsakow, S. S.:Zur Frage der Verpflegung Geisteskranker in der Familie. Allg. Ztschr. f. Psych. 44:274-275, 1888.

Letchworth, W. P.: The Insane in Foreign Countries. G. P. Putnam's Sons, New York, 1889.

Mitchell, Sir Arthur: The Insane Poor in Private Dwellings in Massachusetts. Bost. M. & S. J., 137:457-480, 1897.

Parigot, J.: The Gheel Question: From an American Point of View. Am. Jour. Insanity. 19:332-354, Jan., 1863.

Peeters, J. A.: Present Situation of the Colony of Gheel. Am. Jour. Insanity. 51:539-543, April, 1895.

Pilgrim, C. W.: A Visit to Gheel. Amer. Jour. Insanity. 42:317-327, Jan., 1886.

Pollock, H. M.: Family Care of Mental Patients. Am. Jour. Psychiat. 91:331-336, Sept., 1934.

———: Family Care and the Institutional Problem. PSYCHIAT. QUART. 7:28-36, Jan., 1933.

———: Practical Considerations Relating to Family Care of Mental Patients. Am. Jour. Psychiat. 92:559-564, Nov., 1935.

Prince, E. A.: Colonies for Mental Defectives. Social Hyg. 6:357-364, 1920.

Read, C. S.: Familial Care of the Insane. Jour. Ment. Sci. 67:186-195, 1921.

Roemer, H.:: Der Stand der offenen Geisteskrankenfürsorge in Baden. Allg. Ztschr. f. Psychiat. 88:460-468, April 21, 1928.

Sandy, W. C.: Boarding Out of Mental Patients. Penn. Med. Jour. 39:155-158, Dec., 1935.

Sano, F.: The Care of the Insane Outside of Institutions. Internat. Cong. Ment. Hyg. Proc. 1:379-402, 1930.

——: Des diverses modalités d'assistance hétéro-familiale des aliénés. Ztschr. f. Kinderpsychiat. 2:111-114, Oct., 1935.

Scotland. General Board of Control. Annual report, 1928, 1930, 1931, 1932, 1933, 1934.

Shew, A. M.: The Insane Colony at Gheel. Amer. Jour Insanity. 36:18-27, July, 1879.

Simon, M.: Ein halbes Jahrhundert Familienpflege der Anstalt Ilten. Psychiat.-Neurol. Wochnschr. 36:451-454, Sept. 15, 1934.

Stedman, H. R.: The Family or Boarding-Out Patient System— Its Uses as a Provision for the Insane. Am. Jour. Insanity. 46:327-338, Jan., 1890.

——: The Family System in Practice. Massachusetts State Board of Lunacy and Charity. Annual report, 1888.

Thompson, C. E.: Family Care of the Insane. Amer. Jour. Psychiat. 91:337-352, Sept., 1934.

Tramer, M.: Analyse du rôle psychothérapeutique du placement familial. L'hyg. ment. 28:9-15, Jan., 1933.

van Doninck, A.: Care of Insane at Gheel and Organization of Infirmary. Nederl. tijdschr. v. geneesk. 77:544-551, Feb. 4, 1933.

——: Familial Care of Insane at Gheel: Development of Subdivision Called Winkelomheide. J. Belge de Neurol. et de Psychiat. 33:311-327, April, 1933.

——: Past, Present and Future of Winkelomheide Colony for Familial Care of Insane at Gheel. Psychiat. en Neurol. bl. 37: 563-578, Sept.-Dec., 1933.

van Vleuten, C. F.: Die Familienpflege der Anstalt Dalldorf während und nach dem Kriege. Psychiat.-Neurol. Wochnschr. 23:121, 1921-1922.

Vaux, C. L.: Family Care of Mental Defectives. PSYCHIAT. QUART. 9:349-367, July, 1935.

Vié, J.: Les aspects sociaux de la colonisation hétéro-familiale des aliénés (dans les colonies du type Gheel). J. Belge de Neurol, et de Psychiat. 35:373-380, July, 1935.

——: Les classes d'anormaux dans les colonies familiales d'arriérées. Arch. Internat. de Neurol. 52:1-7, Jan., 1933.

Vié, J., and Chanès: Visiting Nurses of Familial Colonies. Arch. Internat de Neurol. 52:459-468, Nov., 1933.

Wahrendorff: Das Asyl zu Ilten. Allg. Ztschr. f. Psych. 31:679-687, 1875.

——: Über Familienpflege. Allg. Ztschr. f. Psych. 48:405-413, 1891-1892.

Westerterp, M.: Family Care of Nervous and Mental Diseases Subject to Central Observation. Psychiat. en Neurol. bl. 36: 403-417, May-June, 1932.

INDEX

SOCIAL PROBLEMS
AND
SOCIAL POLICY:
The American Experience

An Arno Press Collection

Bachman, George W. and Lewis Meriam. **The Issue of Compulsory Health Insurance.** 1948

Bishop, Ernest S. **The Narcotic Drug Problem.** 1920

Bosworth, Louise Marion. **The Living Wage of Women Workers.** 1911

[Brace, Emma, editor]. **The Life of Charles Loring Brace.** 1894

Brown, Esther Lucile. **Social Work as a Profession.** 4th Edition. 1942

Brown, Roy M. **Public Poor Relief in North Carolina.** 1928

Browning, Grace. **Rural Public Welfare.** 1941

Bruce, Isabel Campbell and Edith Eickhoff. **The Michigan Poor Law.** 1936

Burns, Eveline M. **Social Security and Public Policy.** 1956

Cahn, Frances and Valeska Bary. **Welfare Activities of Federal, State, and Local Governments in California, 1850-1934.** 1936

Campbell, Persia. **The Consumer Interest.** 1949

Davies, Stanley Powell. **Social Control of the Mentally Deficient.** 1930

Devine, Edward T. **The Spirit of Social Work.** 1911

Douglas, Paul H. and Aaron Director. **The Problem of Unemployment.** 1931

Eaton, Allen in Collaboration with Shelby M. Harrison. **A Bibliography of Social Surveys.** 1930

Epstein, Abraham. **The Challenge of the Aged.** 1928

Falk, I[sidore] S., Margaret C. Klem, and Nathan Sinai. **The Incidence of Illness and the Receipt and Costs of Medical Care Among Representative Families.** 1933

Fisher, Irving. **National Vitality, its Wastes and Conservation.** 1909

Freund, Ernst. **The Police Power:** Public Policy and Constitutional Rights. 1904

Gladden, Washington. **Applied Christianity:** Moral Aspects of Social Questions. 1886

Hartley, Isaac Smithson, editor. **Memorial of Robert Milham Hartley.** 1882

Hollander, Jacob H. **The Abolition of Poverty.** 1914

Kane, H[arry] H[ubbell]. **Opium-Smoking in America and China.** 1882

Klebaner, Benjamin Joseph. **Public Poor Relief in America, 1790-1860.** 1951

Knapp, Samuel L. **The Life of Thomas Eddy.** 1834

Lawrence, Charles. **History of the Philadelphia Almshouses and Hospitals from the Beginning of the Eighteenth to the Ending of the Nineteenth Centuries.** 1905

[Massachusetts Commission on the Cost of Living]. **Report of the Commission on the Cost of Living.** 1910

[Massachusetts Commission on Old Age Pensions, Annuities and Insurance]. **Report of the Commission on Old Age Pensions, Annuities and Insurance.** 1910

[New York State Commission to Investigate Provision for the Mentally Deficient]. **Report of the State Commission to Investigate Provision for the Mentally Deficient.** 1915

[Parker, Florence E., Estelle M. Stewart, and Mary Conymgton, compilers]. **Care of Aged Persons in the United States.** 1929

Pollock, Horatio M., editor. **Family Care of Mental Patients.** 1936

Pollock, Horatio M. **Mental Disease and Social Welfare.** 1941

Powell, Aaron M., editor. **The National Purity Congress;** Its Papers, Addresses, Portraits. 1896

The President's Commission on the Health Needs of the Nation. **Building America's Health.** [1952]. Five vols. in two

Prostitution in America: Three Investigations, 1902-1914. 1975

Rubinow, I[saac] M. **The Quest for Security.** 1934

Shaffer, Alice, Mary Wysor Keefer, and Sophonisba P. Breckinridge. **The Indiana Poor Law.** 1936

Shattuck, Lemuel. **Report to the Committee of the City Council Appointed to Obtain the Census of Boston for the Year 1845.** 1846

The State and Public Welfare in Nineteenth-Century America: Five Investigations, 1833-1877. 1975

Stewart, Estelle M. **The Cost of American Almshouses.** 1925

Taylor, Graham. **Pioneering on Social Frontiers.** 1930

[United States Senate Committee on Education and Labor]. **Report of the Committee of the Senate Upon the Relations Between Labor and Capital.** 1885. Four vols.

Walton, Robert P. **Marihuana, America's New Drug Problem.** 1938

Williams, Edward Huntington. **Opiate Addiction.** 1922

Williams, Pierce assisted by Isabel C. Chamberlain. **The Purchase of Medical Care Through Fixed Periodic Payment.** 1932

Willoughby, W[estal] W[oodbury]. **Opium as an International Problem.** 1925

Wisner, Elizabeth. **Public Welfare Administration in Louisiana.** 1930